a collection of **the best**
business quotes

a collection of **the best**

business quotes

First published in Great Britain in 2005

This edition published 2006

Designed by seagulls.net

Printed in Thailand by Imago

The value of e-commerce is not in the e, but in the commerce.

Octavio Paz

One worthwhile task carried to a successful conclusion is better than fifty half-finished tasks.

Bertie Charles Forbes

It is all one to me if a man comes from Sing Sing or Harvard. We hire the man, not his history.

Henry Ford

Running a company on market research is like driving while looking in the rear view mirror.

Anita Roddick

There is nothing more requisite in business than dispatch.

Joseph Addison

The green shoots of economic spring are appearing again.

Norman Lamont

> # Without the right attitude, a business with everything going for it will fail.

Robert Heller

Just as 'location, location, location' defines value in real estate, in business today it's connectivity that equals competitiveness.

Mary J Cronin

It is an immutable law of business that words are words, explanations are explanations, promises are promises – but only performance is reality.

Harold S Geneen

The man who starts out simply with the idea of getting rich won't succeed, you must have a larger ambition.

John D Rockefeller

The avoidance of taxes is the only pursuit that still carries any reward.

John Maynard Keynes

The only things that evolve by themselves in an organisation are disorder, friction and malperformance.

Peter Drucker

The trouble with this business is that the stars keep 90% of the money.

Lord Grade

A dinner lubricates business.

Sir William Scott

I didn't know enough to quit. If I had been technically trained, I would have given up, or probably would never have begun. I was a dreamer, and in search of the gold at the foot of the rainbow. I dared where the wise ones feared to tread.

King C Gillette

All progress is based upon a universal innate desire on the part of every organism to live beyond its income.

Samuel Butler

I knew a trade name must be short, vigorous, incapable of being misspelled to an extent that will destroy its identity, and, in order to satisfy trademark laws, it must mean nothing. The letter K had been a favourite with me – it seemed a strong, incisive sort of a letter.

George Eastman (on choosing 'Kodak' as a trade name)

The difference between failure and success is doing a thing nearly right and doing a thing exactly right.

Edward Simmons

A show of a certain amount of honesty is in any profession or business the surest way to growing rich.

Jean de la Bruyère

A bad reference is as hard to find as a good employee.

Robert Half

Speculation is the romance of trade, and casts contempt upon all its sober realities. It renders the stock-jobber a magician, and the exchange a region of enchantment.

Washington Irving

Where would the Rockefellers be today if sainted old John D had gone on selling short-weight kerosene (paraffin to you) to widows and orphans instead of wisely deciding to mulct the whole country?

S J Perelman

I found that there were these incredibly great people at doing certain things, and you couldn't replace one of these people with fifty average people.

Steve Jobs

Trickle-down theory – the less than elegant metaphor that if one feeds the horse enough oats, some will pass through to the road for the sparrows.

J K Galbraith

To succeed –
Early to bed, early to rise,
Never get tight, and – advertise.
Anonymous (attributed to Dr Scholl)

Like a Goth swaggering around Rome wearing an onyx toilet seat for a collar, he exudes self-confidence.
Clive James (on Rupert Murdoch)

Doing business without advertising is like winking at a girl in the dark. You know what you are doing, but nobody else does.
Steuart Henderson Britt

To err is human but to really foul things up requires a computer.

Anonymous

If at first you don't succeed – you're fired.

Lord Grade

The way to rebuild our corporate world is a blend of both male and female energy.

Terri Bowersock

Statistics are like a bikini. What they reveal is suggestive, but what they conceal is vital.

Aaron Levenstein

Every organisation of today has to build into its very structure the management of change.

Peter F Drucker

In every era, society must strike the right balance between the freedom businesses need to compete for a market share and to make profits and the preservation of family and community values.

Hillary Clinton

There's one blessing only, the source and cornerstone of beatitude – confidence in self.

Seneca

It's a kind of spiritual snobbery that makes people think they can be happy without money.

Albert Camus

All business sagacity reduces itself in the last analysis to a judicious use of sabotage.

Thorstein Veblen

When the praying
does no good,
insurance does help.

Bertolt Brecht

For most people the fantasy is driving around in a big car, having all the chicks you want and being able to pay for it. It always has been, still is, and always will be. Anyone who says it isn't is talking bullshit.

Mick Jagger

Enthusiasm and hard work are indispensable ingredients of achievement. So is stick-to-it-iveness.

Clarence Birdseye

Ginger Rogers

The only way to enjoy anything in this life is to earn it first.

Life is a series of experiences, each one of which makes us bigger, even though sometimes it is hard to realise this.

Henry Ford

We often get in quicker by the back door than the front.

Napoleon

Sure I eat what I advertise. Sure I eat Wheaties for breakfast. A good bowl of Wheaties with Bourbon can't be beat.

Dizzy Dean

A bank is the place where they lend you an umbrella in fair weather and ask for it back when it begins to rain.

Robert Frost

Any customer can have a car painted any colour that he wants so long as it's black.

Henry Ford

No McTavish
Was ever lavish.

Ogden Nash

Accountancy: a profession whose idea of excitement is sharpening a bundle of No. 2 pencils . . .

Anonymous

Do what you can, with what you have, where you are.

Theodore Roosevelt

I probably spend some time once a month listening in on calls or talking to customers. I encourage my executives to do the same.

Lillian Vernon

If it works well, they'll stop making it.

Jane Otten and Russell Baker

The Web will be one more area of significant change and those who don't pay attention will get hurt, while those who see it early enough will get rewarded.

Steve Jobs

How can we sit together and deal with this industry if you're going to do things like this to me? If this is the way you do it, gentlemen, include me out!

Sam Goldwyn

Some see private enterprise as a predatory target to be shot, others as a cow to be milked, but few are those who see it as a sturdy horse pulling a wagon.

Sir Winston Churchill

I buy when other people are selling. **J Paul Getty**

Advertising is a valuable economic factor because it is the cheapest way of selling goods, particularly if the goods are worthless.

Sinclair Lewis

How is a legend different from a brand? An alternative spelling of 'legend' is g-u-t-s.

Harriet Ruben

I am willing to turn an entire company upside down if it's time to do that. We're in perpetual evolution.

Richard Branson

Knowledge is the only meaningful resource today. The traditional 'factors of production' – land (i.e. natural resources), labour and capital – have not disappeared. But they have become secondary.

Peter Drucker

A corporation does seem like a family. Not necessarily that one big happy family they like to boast about … but just like every family, a hotbed of passion, rivalry, and dreams that build or destroy careers.

Paula Bernstein

We can't start talking objectives until we know what they are. The things we desire are not objectives … When you do not figure out the real objectives, you substitute procedure for thinking.

Peter Drucker

One's objective should be to get it right, get it quick, get it out, and get it over ... your problem won't improve with age.

Warren Buffett

A wise man will make more opportunities than he finds.

Francis Bacon

My father taught me to work, but not to love it. I never did like to work, and I don't deny it. I'd rather read, tell stories, crack jokes, talk, laugh – anything but work.

Abraham Lincoln

There is nothing like the ticker tape except a woman – nothing that promises, hour after hour, day after day, such sudden developments; nothing that disappoints so often or occasionally fulfils with such unbelievable, passionate magnificence.

Walter Knowleton Gutman

When a man is trying to sell you
something, don't imagine he is
that polite all the time.
Edgar Watson Howe

IIf you have enough meetings over a
long enough period of time, the meetings
become more important than the problem
the meetings were intended to solve.
Dr E R Hendrickson

Never cheat, but do not be soft. It is a hard
world. Be harder. But, and this is the test, at
the same time, obviously, be a good fellow.
Gerald Sparrow

Why do men delight in work? Fundamentally, I suppose, because there is a sense of relief and pleasure in getting something done — a kind of satisfaction not unlike that which a hen enjoys on laying an egg.

H L Mencken

Every great man has a woman behind him … And every great woman has some man in front of her, tripping her up.

Dorothy L Sayers

The Body Shop fosters a spirit of experimentation and a creative climate in which we produce new products out of old ingredients. We are not afraid to reach into the past, or look at the practices of other cultures, in order to improve what we have here and now – and in the future.

Anita Roddick

A statistician is a person who draws a mathematically precise line from an unwarranted assumption to a foregone conclusion.

Anonymous

Brands are all about trust. You buy the brand because you consider it a friend.

Michael Perry

Business underlies everything in our national life, including our spiritual life. Witness the fact that in the Lord's Prayer the first petition is for daily bread.

Woodrow Wilson

Every young man should have a hobby. Learning how to handle money is the best one. Jack Hurley

B C Forbes

If you don't drive your business you will be driven out of business.

All work and no play makes Jack a dull boy – and Jill a wealthy widow.

Evan Esar

Bad administration, to be
sure, can destroy good policy;
but good administration can
never save bad policy.

Adlai Stevenson

At some time in the life cycle
of virtually every organisation,
its ability to succeed in spite
of itself runs out.

Richard H Brien

I suspect guys who say,
'I just send out for a sandwich
for lunch,' as lazy men trying
to impress me.

Jimmy Cannon

I can't do anything without first putting on lipstick.

Geraldine Laybourne

Creative people are like a wet towel. You wring them out and pick up another one.

Charles Revson

Banking may well be a career from which no man really recovers.

John Kenneth Galbraith

A well-run business must have high and consistent standards of ethics.
Richard Branson

There are few more impressive sights in the world than a Scotsman on the make.
J M Barrie

I'm a brand.
Martha Stewart

There is always an easy solution to every human problem – neat, plausible and wrong.
H L Mencken

Our plans miscarry because we have no aim. When a man does not know what harbour he is making for, no wind is the right wind.
Seneca

If you would know the value of money, go and borrow some.

Benjamin Franklin

Comment is free but facts are on expenses.

Sir Tom Stoppard

It requires a great deal of boldness and a great deal of caution to make a great fortune, and when you have got it, it requires ten times more wit to keep it.

Ralph Waldo Emerson

If you can build a business up big enough, it's respectable.

Will Rogers

Promotion should not be more important than accomplishment, or avoiding instability more important than taking the right risk.

Peter Drucker

I learned then what a bunch of gangsters the banks are. They *really* are gangsters.

Alan Sugar

Total commitment to family and total commitment to career is possible, but fatiguing.

Muriel Fox

Competition brings out the best in products and the worst in people.

David Sarnoff

The world is full of willing people; some willing to work, the rest willing to let them.

Robert Frost

There are
two options:
adapt or die.

Andrew S Grove

I understand. You work very hard two days a week and you need a five-day weekend. That's normal.

Neil Simon

This is not an age of castles, moats and armour where people can sustain a competitive advantage for very long.

Richard D'Aveni

Effort is only effort when it begins to hurt.

José Ortega y Gasset

If God had meant us to travel tourist class,
He would have made us narrower.
Martha Zimmerman

Half the failures in life arise from
pulling in one's horse as he is leaping.
Julius and Augustus Hare

You may not realise it when it happens, but a kick in the teeth may be the best thing in the world for you.

Walt Disney

I feel sorry for those who live without competition … fat, dumb, and unhappy in cradle-to-grave security.

Donald M Kendall

I yield to no one in my admiration for the office as a social centre, but it's no place actually to get any work done.

Katharine Whitehorn

We are not interested in the possibilities of defeat.

Queen Victoria

Wealth is the product of man's capacity to think.

Ayn Rand

Have you ever been out for a late autumn walk in the closing part of the afternoon, and suddenly looked up to realise that the leaves are practically all gone? And the sun has set and the day gone before you knew it – and with that a cold wind blows across the landscape? That's retirement.

Stephen Leacock

The shares are a penny, and ever so many are taken by Rothschild and Baring, And just as a few are allotted to you, you awake with a shudder despairing.

W S Gilbert

It must always be kept in mind that the customer often knows more about the goods than the advertising writers because they have had experience in buying them.

John Wanamaker

It is not always by plugging away at a difficulty and sticking at it that one overcomes it; but, rather, often by working on the one next to it. Certain people and certain things require to be approached on an angle.

André Gide

Advertising is the rattling of a stick
in a swill bucket.
George Orwell

Yesterday is a cancelled cheque; tomorrow
is a promissory note; today is the only cash
you have – so spend it wisely.
Kay Lyons

Will somebody please explain to me
why public relations people are almost
invariably 'associates'? Whom do they
associate with, and who can stand it?
George Dixon

There is no such thing as 'soft sell' and 'hard sell'. There is only 'smart sell' and 'stupid sell'.

Charles Brower

If Max [Lord Beaverbrook] gets to Heaven he won't last long. He will be chucked out for trying to pull off a merger between Heaven and Hell … after having secured a controlling interest in key subsidiary companies in both places, of course.

H G Wells

If all corporations were run like Fininvest, there would be no problems of public morality in Italy.

Silvio Berlusconi

Remember that time is money.
Benjamin Franklin

What's worth doing is worth doing for money.

Joseph Donohue

Our whole economy is based on planned obsolescence.

Brooks Stevens

He who findeth fault meaneth to buy.

Thomas Fuller

The desire for safety stands against every great and noble enterprise.

Tacitus

It is ironic but true that in this era of electronic communications, personal interaction is becoming more important than ever.

Regis McKenna

There is a tide in the affairs of men
Which, taken at the flood, leads on to fortune.

William Shakespeare

We are built to conquer environment, solve problems, achieve goals, and we find no real satisfaction or happiness in life without obstacles to conquer and goals to achieve.

Maxwell Maltz

One can never consent to creep when one feels an impulse to soar.

Helen Keller

A man who has a million dollars is as well off as if he were rich.

John Jacob Astor

The world is first a Coke world, then an orange world, then a lemon-lime world.

Roberto Goizueta

When I want a peerage,
I shall buy it like an honest man.
Lord Northcliffe

In all successful professional groups,
regard for the individual is based
not on title, but on competence,
stature, and leadership.
Marvin Bower

Nothing splendid has ever been
achieved except by those who dared
believe that something inside them
was superior to circumstance.
Bruce Barton

A good ad should be like a good sermon; it must not only comfort the afflicted, it also must afflict the comfortable.

Bernice Fitz-Gibbon

Teenagers travel in droves, packs, swarms. To the librarian, they're a gaggle of geese. To the cook they're a scourge of locusts. To department stores they're a big beautiful exaltation of larks, all lovely and loose and jingly.

Bernice Fitz-Gibbon

The consumer dictates whether we're in business or not.

Niall Fitzgerald

We do the past very well in this country but how can we compete from a high-tech point of view when the rest of the world sees us dressed up in top hats and crinolines all the time?

Roger Puttman

If ambition doesn't hurt you, you haven't got it.

Kathleen Norris

People of the same trade seldom meet together, even for merriment and diversion, but the conversation ends in a conspiracy against the public, or in some contrivance to raise prices.

Adam Smith

Without humanity a man cannot long endure adversity, nor can he long enjoy posterity. Confucius

Shona L Brown

Managing change is about leading change.

If at first you don't succeed, try, try, again. Then quit. There's no use being a damn fool about it.

W C Fields

Monopoly is business at the
end of its journey.

Henry Demarest Lloyd

The cosmetics industry is the
nastiest business in the world.

Elizabeth Arden

Contract: an agreement that is
binding on the weaker party.

Frederick Sawyer

I'd like to live like a poor man
with lots of money.

Pablo Picasso

The toughest thing about being a success is that you've got to keep on being a success.

Irving Berlin

I've been rich and I've been poor; rich is better.

Sophie Tucker

Men are never so tired or harassed as when they have to deal with a woman who wants a raise.
Michael Korda

Nothing is more difficult, and therefore more precious, than to be able to decide.
Napoleon

In a real estate man's eye, the most exclusive part of the city is wherever he has a house to sell.

Will Rogers

The fact that a business is large, efficient and profitable does not mean that it takes advantage of the public.

Charles Clore

The maxim of British people is 'Business as usual'.

Sir Winston Churchill

If you pay peanuts, you get monkeys.

Sir James Goldsmith

I have climbed the greasy pole of success.

Benjamin Disraeli

If the human being is condemned and restricted to perform the same functions over and over again, he will not even be a good ant, not to mention a good human being.

Norbert Wiener

'Don't ask the price, it's a penny'

Slogan hung above Simon Marks' penny bazaars

Statistics indicate that, as a result of over-work, modern executives are dropping like flies on the nation's golf courses.

Ira Wallach

Everyone has a right to work and everyone has the right to pass a picket line.

James Callaghan

One of the greatest pieces of economic wisdom is to know what you do not know.

J K Galbraith

The first springs of great events, like those of great rivers, are often mean and little.

Jonathan Swift

If you don't get it right, what's the point?

Michael Cimino

Only the paranoid survive.

Andrew Grove

The longest word in the English language is the one following the phrase: 'And now a word from our sponsor.'

Hal Eaton

Many a man owes his success to his first wife, and his second wife to his success.

Jim Backus

There's no such thing as a free lunch.

Milton Friedman

The outcome of any serious research
can only be to make two questions
grow where one question grew before.
Thorstein Veblen

If you don't want to work you have to
work to earn enough money so that
you won't have to work.
Ogden Nash

You can't win without being completely different. When everyone else says we are crazy, I say, gee we really must be on to something.

Larry D Ellison

Be not penny-wise: riches have wings, and sometimes they fly away of themselves; sometimes they must be set flying to bring in more.

Francis Bacon

The businessman needs three umbrellas – one to leave at the office, one to leave at home and one to leave on the train.

Paul Dickson

I don't meet competition, I crush it.

Charles Revson

Growth is the only evidence of life.

Cardinal Newman

A man without a smiling face must not open a shop.

Chinese Proverb

I've got a virtually limitless supply of bullshit.

Ted Turner

In democracies, nothing is more great or more brilliant than commerce: it attracts the attention of the public, and fills the imagination of the multitude; all energetic passions are directed towards it.

Alexis de Tocqueville

Question: What's two and two?
Answer: Buying or selling?
Lord Grade

There are poor men in this country who
cannot be bought: the day I found that
out I sent my gold abroad.
Comtesse de Voigrand

The force of the guinea you have in your
pocket depends wholly on the default of the
guinea in your neighbour's pocket. If he did
not want it, it would be of no use to you.
John Ruskin

There are but two ways of paying debt: increase of industry in raising income, increase of thrift in laying out.

Thomas Carlyle

When the client moans and sighs
Make his logo twice the size.
If he still should prove refractory, show a picture of a factory.
Only in the gravest cases
Should you show the clients' faces.

Anonymous

People who work
sitting down get
paid more than
people who work
standing up.

Ogden Nash

Success is a science; if you have the conditions, you get the result.

Oscar Wilde

Dear, never forget one little point. It's my business. You just work here.

Elizabeth Arden (from a note to her husband)

I believe in provocative disruption.

Charlotte Beers

He is the best sailor who can steer within fewest points of the wind, and exact a motive power out of the greatest obstacles.

Henry David Thoreau

You cannot bore people into buying your product. You must interest them into buying it. You cannot save souls in an empty church.

David Ogilvy

One of the saddest things is that the only thing a man can do for eight hours a day, day after day, is work. You can't eat eight hours a day nor drink for eight hours a day nor make love for eight hours.

William Faulkner

Anyone can do any amount of work provided it isn't the work he is supposed to be doing at that moment.

Robert Benchley

The compensation of a very early success is the conviction that life is a romantic matter. In the best sense one stays young.

F Scott Fitzgerald

There are few ways in which a man can be more innocently employed than in getting money.

Samuel Johnson

To succeed at re-engineering,
you have to be a missionary,
a motivator, and a leg breaker.
Michael Hammer

Inflation is the most important fact
of our time, the single greatest peril
to our economic health.
Bernard M Baruch

It used to be that people needed
products to survive. Now products
need people to survive.
Nicholas Johnson

Let a man start out in life to build something better and sell it cheaper than it has been built or sold before, let him have that determination and the money will roll in.

Henry Ford

The man who is denied the opportunity of taking decisions of importance begins to regard as important the decisions he is allowed to take.

C Northcote Parkinson

The most important thing in business is to have an organisation that works together, and the key question in computing is to be able to tie up machines easily with each other.

Ken Olsen

One of the lessons from the Darwinian world is that the excellence of an organism's nervous system helps determine its ability to sense change and quickly respond, thereby surviving or even thriving.

Bill Gates

Men in general judge more from appearances than from reality. All men have eyes, but few have the gift of penetration.

Machiavelli

'How doth the busy bee improve each shining hour, and gather honey all the day from every opening flower.' Well, he does not. He spends most of the day in buzzing and aimless aerobatics, and gets about a fifth of the honey he would collect if he organised himself.

Sir Heneage Ogilvie

If a woman is sufficiently ambitious, determined and gifted – there is practically nothing she can't do.
Helen Lawrenson

Sir Montague Burton

A business must have a conscience as well as a counting house.

Never ask of money spent

Where the spender thinks it went.

Nobody was ever meant

To remember or invent

What he did with every cent.

Robert Frost

Airline travel is hours of boredom
interrupted by moments of stark terror.

Al Boliska

Spending one's own capital is feeding a dog on his own tail.

Mark Twain

The reward of energy, enterprise and thrift – is taxes.

William Feather

Few bosses would tell a male clerk to brew up a pot of tea.

John Forrester

Money is better than poverty, if only for financial reasons.

Woody Allen

A fair price for oil is whatever you can get plus ten per cent.

Dr Ali Ahmed Attiga

Work expands to fill the time available for its completion.

C Northcote Parkinson

A self-made man is one who believes in luck and sends his son to Oxford.

Christina Stead

The oppressive atmosphere in most companies resembles downtown Calcutta in summer.

Christopher Bartlett

They have not any difficulties on the way up because they fly, but they have many when they reach the summit.

Niccolò Machiavelli

A young man must let his ideas grow, not be continually rooting them up to see how they are getting on.

William McFee

A prosperous competitor is often less dangerous than a desperate one.

Barry J Nalebuff

He who wields the knife never wears the crown.

Michael Heseltine

A small loan makes a debtor; a great one, an enemy.

Publilius Syrus

The heroic role of the captain of industry is that of a deliverer from an excess of business management. It is the casting out of businessmen by the chief of businessmen.

Thorstein Veblen

But think how early I go!

Lord Castlerose (on arriving late at his job in the City)

If you have any money in that place [The Knickerbocker Trust Company], get it out first thing tomorrow. The men in that bank are too good-looking.

Hetty Green (The Witch of Wall Street)

A man who has no office to go to – I don't care who he is – is a trial of which you can have no conception.

George Bernard Shaw

What we do during our working hours determines what we have; what we do in our leisure hours determines what we are.

George Eastman

It is well known what a middle man is: he is a man who bamboozles one party and plunders the other.

Benjamin Disraeli

The avoidance of tax may be lawful, but it is not yet a virtue.

Lord Denning

The achiever is the only person who is truly alive.

George Allen

The hotel is full of spies, impoverished grandees and nondescript people, including Rothschilds down to their last two millions.

Chips Channon

Advertising may be described as the science of arresting the human intelligence long enough to get money from it.

Stephen Leacock

It takes twenty years to make an overnight success.

Eddie Cantor

Advertising in the final analysis should be news. If it is not news it is worthless.

Adolph S Ochs

The worst crime against working people is a company which fails to operate at a profit.

Samuel Gompers

The business world worships mediocrity. Officially we revere free enterprise, initiative and individuality. Unofficially we fear it.

George Lois

The most likely place to have your idea pocket-picked is at a meeting … Here an idea becomes public property the moment it hits the airwaves.

Jane Trahey

It is well for a man to respect his own vocation whatever it is and to think himself bound to uphold it and to claim for it the respect it deserves.

Charles Dickens

He's spending a year dead for tax reasons.

Douglas Adams

Nothing is illegal if 100 businessmen decide to do it.

Andrew Young

Hiccups in the international business scene are not new to us. Wedgwood china has survived upheavals before – the Napoleonic Wars, the Franco-Prussian War, the world wars.

Arthur Bryan

Everyone has a button. If enough people have the same button you have a successful ad and a successful product.

Jerry Della Femina

We even sell a pair of earrings for under £1, which is cheaper than a prawn sandwich from Marks & Spencer. But I have to say the earrings probably won't last as long.

Gerald Ratner

The secret of success in life, and consequently of making money, is to enjoy your work. If you do, nothing is hard work – no matter how many hours you put in.

Billy Butlin

The customer is always right.
H Gordon Selfridge

When men are rightly occupied, their amusement grows out of their work.
John Ruskin

How to be an efficient secretary is to develop the kind of self-abnegating sacrificial instincts usually possessed only by the early saints on their way to martyrdom.
Jill Tweedie

One man that has a mind and knows it can always beat ten men who haven't and don't.

George Bernard Shaw

If you can avoid a decision, do so. If you can get somebody else to avoid a decision, don't avoid it yourself. If you cannot get one person to avoid a decision, appoint a committee.

Attributed to Sharu S Ragnekar

In order to be irreplaceable one must always be different.

Coco Chanel

He uses statistics as a drunken man uses lamp posts – for support rather than illumination. Andrew Lang

Eighty percent of success is showing up.

Woody Allen

Not having to worry about money is almost like not having to worry about dying.

Mario Puzo

Avis Rent-a-Car slogan: 'We're number two, we try harder'.

Robert Townsend

Few things tend more to alienate friendship than a want of punctuality in our engagements.

William Hazlitt

A man has one hundred dollars and you leave him with two dollars, that's subtraction.

Mae West

Money is God in Action.

Frederick J Eikerenkoetter II ('Reverend Ike')

I think that business practices would improve immeasurably if they were guided by 'feminine' principles – qualities like love and care and intuition.

Buzz Kennedy

I have yet to hear a man ask for advice on how to combine marriage and a career.

Gloria Steinem

The advanced economy could not run for thirty seconds without computers.

Alvin Toffler

She's the kind of girl who climbed the ladder of success, wrong by wrong.

Mae West

When you get right down to the root of
the meaning of the word 'succeed' you find
that it simply means to follow through.
F W Nichol

A young Scotsman of your ability let loose
upon the world with £300, what would he
not do? It's almost appalling to think of;
especially if he went among the English.
J M Barrie

Money can't buy you happiness
but you can be miserable in comfort.
Anonymous

It is a socialist idea that making profits is a vice; I consider the real vice is making losses.

Sir Winston Churchill

The single most important determinant of corporate culture is the behaviour of the chief executive officer. He or she is the one clearly responsible for shaping the beliefs, motives, commitments, and predispositions of all.

Warren Bennis

A budget tells us what we can't afford, but it doesn't keep us from buying it.

William Feather

The world is divided into people who do things and people who get the credit. Try, if you can, to belong to the first class. There's less competition.

Dwight Morrow

What one generation sees as a luxury, the next sees as a necessity.

Anthony Crosland

Nothing that you will learn in the course of your studies will be of the slightest possible use to you in after life – save only this – that if you work hard and intelligently you should be able to detect when a man is talking rot, and that, in my view, is the main, if not the sole, purpose of education.

J A Smith

He that would have the fruit must climb the tree.
Thomas Fuller

The secret of success is sincerity. Once you can fake that you've got it made.

Arthur Bloch

Do your work with your whole heart and you will succeed – there is so little competition!

Elbert Hubbard

Chief executives seem no more able to resist their biological urge to merge, than dogs can resist chasing rabbits.

Philip Coggan

You have not done enough, you have never done enough, so long as it is possible that you have something to contribute.

Dag Hammarskjöld

I learned the value of counter footage, that is, that each counter foot of space had to pay the wages, rent, overhead expenses, and earn a profit.

Simon Marks

There is no security on this earth; there is only opportunity.

General MacArthur

Success is a journey, not a destination.

Ben Sweetland

One man's pay increase is another man's price increase.

Harold Wilson

It's a recession when your neighbour loses his job: it's a depression when you lose yours.
Harry S Truman

The distinctive function of the banker begins as soon as he uses the money of others.
David Ricardo

Money is like manure. If you spread it
around it does a lot of good, but if you
pile it up in one place it stinks like hell.
Clint Murchinson

People want economy and they
will pay any price to get it.
Lee Iacocca

One doesn't discover new lands
without consenting to lose sight
of the shore for a very long time.
André Gide

Real power is creating stuff.

Geraldine Laybourne

Chaplin is no businessman – all he knows is that he can't take anything less.

Sam Goldwyn

After you've done a thing the same way for two years, look it over carefully. After five years, look at it with suspicion. And after ten years, throw it away and start over.

Alfred Edward Perlman

It's just like having a licence to print your own money.

Attributed to Lord Thomson of Fleet (on the subject of commercial television)

The philosophy behind much advertising is based on the old observation that every man is really two men – the man he is, and the man he wants to be.

William Feather

You must accept that if the computer is a tool, it is the job of the tool user to know what to use it for.

Peter F Drucker

It is idle to speak of organisational transformation without individuals being transformed, especially the leader.

S K Chakraborty

Nothing focuses the mind better than the constant sight of a competitor who wants to wipe you off the map.

Wayne Calloway

The dictionary is the only place where success comes before work.

Arthur Brisbane

Work is more fun than fun.

Trammell Crow

A banker is a person who is willing to make a loan if you present him with sufficient evidence to show you don't need it.

Herbert V Prochnow

Do not think a man has done his full duty when he has performed the work assigned him. A man will never rise if he does only this.

Andrew Carnegie

Do other men for they would do you. That's the true business precept.

Charles Dickens

It is not the employer who pays wages – he only handles the money. It is the product that pays wages.

Henry Ford

Leadership, like swimming, cannot be learned by reading about it.

Henry Mintzberg

Advertising is merely a substitute for a personal sales force – an extension, if you will, of the merchant who cried about his wares.

Rosser Reeves

Experience has taught me this, that we undo ourselves by impatience. Misfortunes have their life and their limits, their sickness and their health.

Michel de Montaigne

While the work or play is on, it is a lot of fun if while you are doing one you don't constantly feel that you ought to be doing the other.

Franklin P Adams

I hadn't been in the hotel business five minutes before I knew this was *it*.

Conrad Hilton

Even the frankest and bravest of subordinates do not talk to their boss the same way they talk with colleagues.

Robert Greenleaf

Money it turned out, was exactly like sex, you thought of nothing else if you didn't have it and thought of other things if you did.

James Baldwin

Soon the emphasis will be on getting a life instead of a career, and work will be viewed as a series of gigs or projects.

Jonas Ridderstråle

If I wanted to get anything out of this business [rock music] it was never to have to go back and work in a factory again.

Roger Daltrey

The software industry as a whole
tends to be slightly managed chaos.
Ann Winblad

Nobody here [Apple Computers]
cares which washroom you use.
Debi Coleman

To get profit without risk, experience
without danger, and reward without
work, is as impossible as it is to live
without being born.
A P Gouthey

A good secretary can save her boss more time in a year than a business jet plane can.

Malcolm Baldridge

You ask me what it is I do. Well actually, you know,
I'm partly a liaison man and partly P.R.O.
Essentially I integrate the current export drive
And basically I'm viable from ten o'clock till five.

John Betjeman

Anybody can cut prices, but it takes a brain to produce a better article.

P D Armour

To be brave in misfortune is to be worthy of manhood; to be wise in misfortune is to conquer fate. Agnes Repplier

Happiness seems to require a modicum of external prosperity. **Aristotle**

Power is the ability to get things done.

Rosabeth Moss Kanter

When the product is right, you don't have to be a great marketer.

Lee Iacocca

Nothing defines human beings better than their willingness to do irrational things in the pursuit of phenomenally unlikely payoffs.

Scott Adams

I like work: it fascinates me. I can sit and look at it for hours. I love to keep it by me: the idea of getting rid of it nearly breaks my heart.

Jerome K Jerome

I don't have ulcers, I give them.

Harry Cohn

To take full advantage of the potential in e-business, leaders must think differently, and people must work together differently. Let's call this new way of working e-culture – the human side of the global information era.

Rosabeth Moss Kanter

There is nothing Japan really wants to buy from foreign countries except, possibly, neckties with unusual designs.

Yoshihiro Inayama

Accountants are the witch-doctors of the modern world and willing to turn their hands to any kind of magic.

Lord Justice Harman

Today's global economic dance is no Strauss waltz. It's break dancing accompanied by street rap.

Tom Peters

It is most important in this world to be
pushing, but it is fatal to seem so.
Benjamin Jowett

If figures of speech based on sports and
fornication were suddenly banned,
American corporate communication would
be reduced to pure mathematics.

Jay McInerney

Crime is the logical extension of the sort of
behaviour that is often considered perfectly
respectable in legitimate business.

Robert Rice

It is the characteristic excellence of the strong man that he can bring momentous issues to the fore and make a decision about them. The weak are always forced to decide between alternatives they have not chosen for themselves.

Dietrich Bonhoeffer

No matter how lofty you are in your department, the responsibility for what your lowliest assistant is doing is yours.

Bessie Rowland James

In the middle of a hard project, I remind people to do something else. Sometimes people need to work on something completely different to get their best ideas.

Brad Fregger

If you are having as much fun running a big corporation as you did running a piece of it, then you are probably interfering too much with the people who really make it happen.

James Burke

No bird soars too high,
if he soars with his
own wings.

William Blake

America is still a place where most people react to seeing a
man in a Ferrari by redoubling their own efforts to be able
to afford one, rather than by trying to let down his tyres.

Anonymous

Women are ... running their businesses on what
we call the familial model, a family, instead of a
hierarchical top-down military model.

Faith Popcorn

Mark McCormack

Never pick up someone else's ringing phone.

A stockbroker is someone who takes all your money and invests it until it's gone.

Woody Allen

People don't choose their careers. They are engulfed by them.

John Dos Passos

Faint heart never won fair lady or sold any life insurance.

Frank McKinney Hubbard

Like a force of nature, the digital age cannot be denied or stopped.

Nicholas Negroponte

The only reason to invest in a market is because you think you know something others don't. R Foster Winans

We're overpaying him – but he's worth it.

Sam Goldwyn

No one wins a sales promotion war.

Don E Schultz

It is impossible to win the race unless you venture to run, impossible to win the victory unless you dare to battle.
Richard M DeVos

True learning begins with unlearning.
Fred Kofman

With money in your pocket,
you are wise and handsome
and you sing well too.

Jewish saying

I believe that work is a combination
of emotion and reason and you should
never exclude how you feel from your
decision-making process.

Tamara Ingram

Most people live and die with their music
still unplayed. They never dare to try.

Mary Kay Ash

For exercise, I wind my watch.

Robert Maxwell

I studied the lives of great men and famous women, and I found that the men and women who got to the top were those who did the jobs they had in hand, with everything they had of energy and enthusiasm and hard work.

Harry S Truman

Launching your own business is like writing your own personal declaration of independence from the corporate beehive.

Paula Nelson

Investing is a business that never tires. You have to work with every known thing in the world – the weather in Asia, or politics in East Europe, or the scandal of an American president.

Charles Brady

A plumber's idea of Cleopatra.

W C Fields on Mae West

I have no complex about wealth. I have worked hard for my money, producing things people need. I believe that the able industrial leader who creates wealth and employment is more worthy of historical notice than politicians and soldiers.

J Paul Getty

We believe that a customer should have a choice of different ways to shop.

Charles Dunstone

If you think morality is a luxury business can't afford, try living in a world without it.

Anita Roddick

The real problem is not whether machines think but whether men do.

B F Skinner

Experience is the name everyone gives to their mistakes.

Oscar Wilde

Don't sell the steak; sell the sizzle.

Elmer Wheeler

I find it rather easy to portray a businessman. Being bland, rather cruel and incompetent comes naturally to me.

John Cleese

You just have to be the kind of guy to get people to do things.

Donald J Trump

Europe's strength is its diversity, not its uniformity.

Sir John Harvey-Jones

It takes little talent to see clearly what lies under one's nose, a good deal of it to know in what direction to point that organ.

W H Auden

If Patrick Henry thought that taxation without representation was bad, he should see how bad it is with representation.

Anonymous

There is no excuse. If they don't get the target, they don't get their bonus – we have no discussions.

Liisa Joronen

If an executive does not have time for ostentatious spending, his wife or children will do it for him.

Jorge Luis Borges

People who reach the top of the tree are only those who haven't got the qualifications to detain them at the bottom.

Peter Ustinov

There is only one valid definition of business:

to create a customer.

Peter F Drucker

Men are quite humourless about their own businesses.

Betty MacDonald

We may be in a rapidly evolving international financial system with all the bells and whistles of the so-called new economy. But the old-economy rules of prudence are as formidable as ever. We violate them at our own peril.

Alan Greenspan

Owning the intellectual property is like owning land: you need to keep investing in it again and again to get a payoff. You can't simply sit back and collect the rent.

Esther Dyson

Lifelong learners take risks. Much more than others, these men and women push themselves out of their comfort zones and try new ideas.

Bob Guccione

If you want to see the future, go to an industry confab and get a list of what was talked about. Then ask, 'What did people never talk about?' That's where you're going to find opportunity.

Gary Hamel

I found that when I did as well as the
men in the field, I got more credit for
my work because I am a woman,
which seems unfair.
Eugenie Clark

**Failing is a learning experience. It can be
a gravestone or a stepping stone.**
Bud Hadfield

I could buy companies, tart up their
products and put my name on them,
but I don't want to do that. That's
what our competitors do.
James Dyson

The new electronic interdependence recreates the world in the image of a global village.

Marshall McLuhan

A company needs smart young men with the imagination and the guts to turn everything upside down if they can. It also needs old figures to keep them from turning upside down those things that ought to be rightside up.

Henry Ford

There is no gap in the market unless you have sharp elbows.

Andrew Neil

For a salesman, there is no rock bottom to the life …
A salesman is got to dream, boy. It goes with the territory.
Arthur Miller

Invention is the mother of necessity.

Thorstein Veblen

You're either part of the solution or part of the problem.

Eldridge Cleaver

Microsoft is always just two years away from failure.

Bill Gates

The leader must know, must know that he knows, and must be able to make it abundantly clear to those about him that he knows.

Clarence B Randall

A couple of hours in a hot kitchen can teach you as much about management as the latest books on re-engineering or total quality management.

Tom Peters

The only people in the whole world who can change things are those who can sell ideas.

Lois Wyse

If one is on the spot, disorders are seen as they spring up, and one can quickly remedy them; but if one is not at hand, they are heard of only when they are great and then one can no longer remedy them.

Niccolò Machiavelli

All the guys I knew when they were so young and cute have become the Establishment. Especially Mr Gates.

Esther Dyson

A negotiator should observe everything. You must be part Sherlock Holmes, part Sigmund Freud.

Victor Kiam

The pyramid, the chief organisational principle of the modern organisation, turns a business into a traffic jam.

Ricardo Semler

Nothing is really work unless you would
rather be doing something else.
J M Barrie

No other technique for the conduct of life
attaches the individual so firmly to reality as
laying emphasis on work; for his work at
least gives him a secure place in a portion of
reality, in the human community.
Sigmund Freud

Cessation of work is not accompanied by
cessation of expenses.
Cato the Elder

Deals are my art form. Other people paint beautifully on canvas or write wonderful poetry. I like making deals, preferably big deals. That's how I get my kicks.

Donald Trump

The danger is that people can fall in love with the business they're in and get mesmerised by it. As a result, they don't actually see the business.

Allen Sheppard

Money-getters are the benefactors of our race. To them ... are we indebted for our institutions of learning, and of art, our academies, colleges and churches.

P T Barnum

The people who get on in this world are the people who get up and look for the circumstances they want, and, if they can't find them, make them.

George Bernard Shaw

Take care to sell your
horse before it dies.
The art of life is
passing losses on.

Robert Frost

The heights by great men reached and kept
Were not attained by sudden flight,
But they, while their companions slept,
Were toiling upward in the night.

Henry Wadsworth Longfellow

Above all, we wish to avoid having a dissatisfied customer. We consider our customers a part of our organisation. L L Bean

He wishes not to seem, but to be, the best.

Aeschylus

In order to sell your product, you don't so much point out its merits as you first work like hell to sell yourself.

Louis Kronenberger

Television: The word is
half Greek, half Latin.
No good can come of it.

C P Scott

When the wind of change
blows, some build walls,
others build windmills.

Anonymous

Business is becoming more
and more akin to intellectual
sumo wrestling.

Sir John Harvey-Jones

A speech is like a love affair.
Any fool can start it,
but to end it requires considerable skill.

Lord Mancroft

To achieve great things
we must live as though we
were never going to die.

Marquis de Vauvenargues

> In some circumstances, a refusal to be defeated is a refusal to be educated.

Margaret Halsey

You gain strength, courage and confidence by every experience in which you really stop to look fear in the face.
Eleanor Roosevelt

The really idle man gets nowhere. The perpetually busy man does not get much further.
Sir Heneage Ogilvie

Anytime you have a fiercely competitive, change-oriented growth business where results count and merit matters, women will rise to the top.

Carly Fiorina

Creativity is never enough.

Adrienne Landau

Good decisions come from wisdom. Wisdom comes from experience. Experience comes from bad decisions.

Anonymous

In economics the majority is always wrong.

J K Galbraith

Property is the fruit of labour; property is desirable; it is a positive good.

Abraham Lincoln

Compared to what we ought to be, we are only half awake. We are making use of only a small part of our physical and mental resources. Stating the thing broadly, the human individual thus lives far within his limits.

William James

Every company has two organisational structures: The formal one is written on the charts; the other is the everyday relationships of the men and women in the organisation.

Harold S Geneen

To be successful, keep looking tanned, live in an elegant building (even if you're in the cellar), be seen in smart restaurants (even if you nurse one drink) and if you borrow, borrow big.

Aristotle Onassis

Three components make an entrepreneur: the person, the idea and the resources to make it happen.

Anita Roddick

The best balance of morale for employee productivity can be described this way: happy, but with low self-esteem.

Scott Adams

It saves a lot of trouble if, instead of having to earn money and save it, you just go and borrow it.

Sir Winston Churchill

Most large markets evolve from niche markets.

Regis McKenna

I dream for a living.

Steven Spielberg

To live means to have something definite to do – a mission to fulfil – and in the measure in which we avoid setting our life to something, we make it empty.

José Ortega y Gasset

I learned more about managing people when I was captain of the rugby team than when I was working for Procter & Gamble.

Jack Rowell

Always be smart enough to hire people brighter than yourself.

Caroline Marland

That's the definition of business, something goes through, something else doesn't. Make use of one, forget the other.

Henry Becque

A friendship founded on business is better than a business founded on friendship.

John D Rockefeller

One of the qualities I always seek in marketing people is curiosity.

Raoul Pinnell

Executive: A man who can make quick decisions and is sometimes right.

Frank McKinney Hubbard

Some are born great, some achieve greatness, and some hire public relations officers.

Daniel J Boorstin

The two most beautiful words in the English language are 'Cheque Enclosed'.

Dorothy Parker

Goals too clearly defined can become blinkers.

Mary Catherine Bateson

When the rate of change outside exceeds the rate of change inside, the end is in sight.

Jack Welch

The average employee can deliver far more than his or her current job demands.

Tom Peters

People are unlikely to know that they need a product which does not exist and the basis of market research in new and innovative products is limited in this regard.

Sir John Harvey-Jones

No less than war or statecraft, the history of Economics has its heroic ages.

Aldous Huxley

If A is a success in life, then A equals x plus y plus z. Work is x; y is play; and z is keeping your mouth shut.

Albert Einstein

There's only one way to find out if a man is honest – ask him. If he says, 'Yes', you know he is a crook.

Groucho Marx

All things start in California and spread to New Jersey, then to London and then throughout Europe.

Stelios Haji-Ioannou

Commuter – one who spends his life
In riding to and from his wife;
A man who shaves and takes a train
And then rides back to shave again.

E B White

What we call luck is the
inner man externalised.
We make things
happen to us.

Robertson Davies

Ghengis Khan was not exactly loveable,
but I suppose he is my favourite historical
character because he was damned efficient.
Kerry Packer

The buck stops
with the guy who
signs the cheques.

Rupert Murdoch

No one can make you feel inferior without your consent.

Eleanor Roosevelt

He is a self-made man and worships his creator.

John Bright

The worst disease which can afflict business executives in their work is not, as popularly supposed, alcoholism; it's egotism.

Harold S Geneen

When I've had a rough day, before I go to sleep I ask myself if there's anything more I can do right now. If there isn't, I sleep sound.

L L Colbert

Competition is warfare.

Andrew S Grove

The capacity to exercise a relatively high degree of imagination, ingenuity, and creativity in the solution of organisational problems is widely, not narrowly, distributed in the population.

Douglas McGregor

I want all our people to believe they are working for the best agency in the world. A sense of pride works wonders.

David Ogilvy

The new source of power is not money in the hands of the few, but information in the hands of the many.

W W Rostow

We have turned our attention to men because we feel that they need it, although some of them may not know it yet.

Anita Roddick

The wild, the absurd, the seemingly crazy:
this kind of thinking is where new ideas
come from ... Staying a child isn't easy.
Nicholas Negroponte

A bad decision is when you know
what to do and you don't do it.
Duncan Goodhew

One of the soundest rules to remember
when making forecasts in the field of
economics is that whatever is to
happen is happening already.
Sylvia Porter

Attempt easy tasks as if they were difficult, and difficult as if they were easy: in the one case that confidence may not fall asleep, in the other that it may not be dismayed.

Baltasar Gracián

I have never seen any rich people. Very often I have thought that I have found them. But it turned out that it was not so. They were not rich at all. They were quite poor. They were hard up. They were pushed for money. They didn't know where to turn for ten thousand dollars.

Stephen Leacock

There is not one shred of evidence that the Internet has had any downward influence on North American or European newspaper circulation.

Conrad Black

If the Wright brothers were alive today, Wilbur would have to fire Orville to reduce costs.

Charles Horton Cooley

You are always going to have people who copy things that work.

Jay S Walker

A new idea is delicate. It can be killed by a sneer or a yawn; it can be stabbed to death by a quip and worried to death by a frown on the right man's brow.

Charles Brower

If a man has money, it is usually a sign, too, that he knows how to take care of it; don't imagine his money is easy to get simply because he has plenty of it. Edgar Watson Howe

Ken Olsen

One company, one strategy, one message.

It's just as sure a recipe for failure to have the right idea fifty years too soon as five years too late.

J R Platt

What a man dislikes in his superiors, let him not display in the treatment of his inferiors.

Tsang Sin

There are two times in a man's life when he should not speculate: when he can't afford it and when he can.

Mark Twain

Changing the direction of a large company is like trying to turn an aircraft carrier. It takes a mile before anything happens.

Al Ries

It is better to underpromise and overdeliver than vice versa.

Narayana Murthy

I think consensus is a poor substitute for leadership.

Charlotte Beers

A financier is a pawnbroker with imagination.

Sir Arthur Wing Pinero

The search button on the browser no longer provides an objective search, but a commercial one.
Tim Berners-Lee

Intense decentralisation … gives managers the freedom usually reserved for entrepreneurs.
James W Farnell

I consider that I am a
revolutionary socialist.
Tiny Rowlands

You show me a capitalist,
I'll show you a bloodsucker.
Malcolm X

An overburdened, stretched executive
is the best executive, because he or
she doesn't have time to meddle, to
deal in trivia, to bother people.
Jack Welch

Pound for pound, Sweden probably has more good managers than any other country.

Jack Welch

Business has to be a force for social change.

Anita Roddick

Globalisation is an opportunity. Well managed, it will help drive forward efforts to build prosperity and eliminate poverty. Badly managed it will increase the divide between rich and poor.

Peter Hain

The safest way to double your money is to fold it over once and put it in your pocket.

Frank McKinney Hubbard

Innovation will always be a mixture of serendipity, genius, and sheer bull-mindedness. But while you can't bottle lightning, you can build lightning rods.

Gary Hamel

As in the instances of alchemy, astrology, witchcraft, and other such popular creeds, political economy has a plausible idea at the root of it.

John Ruskin

'Organisational values' always derive from 'individual values' – especially those of the founding fathers and of the very top executives.

S K Chakraborty

Make your company stock a consumer product. When consumers buy stock in your company, they'll never buy a competitive product.

Faith Popcorn

I'm a great believer in luck, and I find the harder I work the more I have of it.

Thomas Jefferson

Never invest in any ideas you can't illustrate with a crayon.

Peter Lynch

The car, the furniture, the wife, the children – everything has to be disposable. Because you see, the main thing today is shopping.

Arthur Miller

The kinds of people we employ are not afraid of taking risks. If someone mucks up, they don't get a bollocking from me. They know they've mucked up and they redouble their efforts.

Richard Branson

Nothing astonishes men so much as common sense and plain dealing.

Ralph Waldo Emerson

It is not enough to take steps which may some day lead to a goal; each step must be itself a goal and a step likewise.

Goethe

Managing is getting paid for home runs someone else hits.

Casey Stengel

Few things help an individual more than to place responsibility upon him, and to let him know that you trust him.

Booker T Washington

When I find an employee who turns out to be wrong for the job, I feel it is my fault because I made the decision to hire him.

Akio Morita

Debt is like a crazy aunt we keep down in the basement. All the neighbours know she's there, but nobody wants to talk about her.

H Ross Perot

If you can't enjoy consuming it,

you can't work in it.

Michael Grade

My dears, we have not yet touched on the sordid topic of coin …

Joyce Grenfell

In the end we are all sacked and it's always awful. It is as inevitable as death following life. If you are elevated there comes a day when you are demoted.

Alan Clark

Transformational leadership is dynamic leadership in the sense that the leaders throw themselves into a relationship with followers who feel elevated by it and often become more active themselves.

James MacGregor Burns

It used to bug the hell out of me when I'd drop out of the bidding for something and then get a call from a reporter asking, 'So, Mr Trump, how does it feel to get beat?'

Donald J Trump

The historical data support one conclusion with unusual force: *To invest with success, you must be a long-term investor.*

John Clifton Bogle

If you want to sell 'em fish, sell 'em big fish.
That's the secret of success.
Jack Solomons

I finally know what distinguishes man from the other beasts: financial worries.

Jules Renard

The Japanese do not consider work a form of economic activity. Rather, believing that there can be no work which is not a form of religious devotion, they approach everything as a discipline akin to the practice of Zen.

Shichihei Yamamoto

A banker is a man who lends another man the money of a third man.

Guy de Rothschild

We are continually faced by great opportunities brilliantly disguised as insoluble problems. Lee Iacocca

Our mission tritely is to change the world.

Donna Dubinsky

Get me inside any boardroom and I'll get any decision I want.

Alan Bond

Don't say 'Yes' until I finish talking!

Darryl F Zanuck

I get a tremendous charge out of business. I get the same sort of feeling that women must have when their babies pop out.

Sir Terence Conran

We thought the creation and operation of websites was mysterious Nobel Prize stuff, the province of the wild-eyed and purple-haired.

Jack Welch

A loose grip around the throat.

Allen Sheppard (describing his style of management)

The individuals best prepared to succeed are those who can learn, modify, and grow, regardless of age, experience, or ego.

Danny Goodman

One must choose, in life, between making money and spending it. There's no time to do both.

Edouard Bourdet

Strategic planning can neither provide creativity nor deal with it when it emerges by other means.

Henry Mintzberg

The world continues to offer glittering prizes to those who have stout hearts and sharp swords.

F E Smith

In developing our industrial strategy for the period ahead, we have had the benefit of much experience. Almost everything has been tried at least once.

Tony Benn

Public speaking is like the winds of the desert: it blows constantly without doing any good.

King Faisal

My theory is that good furniture could be priced so that the man with a flat wallet could be attracted to it.

Ingvar Kamprad (founder of IKEA)

Not a single, substantial, commercially successful project had come from an adequately funded team. They'd always come from the scrounging, scrapping, under-funded teams.

Ken Olsen

This is the age of intellectual capital, and the most valuable parts of jobs are the human tasks: sensing, judging, creating, building relationships.

Thomas A Stewart

In many of our huge corporations we treat people like commodities. And people cannot be managed. Inventories can be managed, but people must be led.

H Ross Perot

We in the free world can do great things. We proved it in Japan by changing the image of 'made in Japan' from something shoddy to something fine.

Akio Morita

Coming up with an idea should be like sitting on a pin – it should make you jump up and do something.

Kemmons Wilson

When Britain is about to enter the EEC it is somewhat tactless to print on the back of the £5 note a picture of British gunners blowing the French army to blazes and accompanying it with a large portrait of the Duke of Wellington.

Lord Leatherland

When I hear a rich man described as a colourful character I figure he's a bum with money. Jimmy Cannon

Dianna Feinstein

Toughness doesn't have to come in a pinstripe suit.

Human beings,
unfortunately,
tend to respond
to negative
incentives – such
as dismissal.

John P Young

Profit in business comes from repeat customers; customers that boast about your product and service, and that bring friends with them.

W Edwards Deming

He who would learn to fly one day must first learn to stand and walk and run and climb and dance: one cannot fly into flying.

Friedrich Nietzsche

What do you want from me? Fine writing? Or would you like to see the goddam sales curve stop going down and start going up?

Rosser Reeves

I do not love the money. What I do love is the getting of it.

Philip D Armour

Only a fool holds out for the top dollar.

Jospeph P Kennedy

If you've got 'em by the balls, their hearts and minds will follow.

Attributed to The Green Berets

There are few sorrows, however poignant, in which a good income is of no avail.
Logan Pearsall Smith

Money is useful to keep the dogs at bay and the water out.
Richard Adams

Men count up the faults of
those who keep them waiting.

French Proverb

Live together like brothers
and do business like strangers.

Arabic Proverb

Television has … lifted the
manufacture of banality out of the
sphere of handicraft and placed it in
that of a major industry.

Nathalie Sarraute

Never check an interesting fact.

Howard Hughes

Big business could do business anywhere.

Amadeo Giannini

I think that no matter how long a meeting goes on, the best ideas always come during the final five minutes, when people drop their guard and I ask them what they really think.

Michael Eisner

If you would hit the mark, you must aim a little above it;
Every arrow that flies feels the attraction of earth.

Henry Wadsworth Longfellow

In the rarefied air of the media, a single misstep separates sitting on top of the world from standing in the unemployment line.

Harriet Rubin

It seemed that the human being was forever debarred from rational understanding as to why they worked.

Frederick Herzberg

If the Lord had meant us to pay income tax, He'd have made us smart enough to prepare the return.

Kirk Kirkpatrick

Many speak the truth when they say that they despise riches, but they mean the riches possessed by other men.

Charles Caleb Colton

> # Praise should always be given in public, criticism should always be given in private.

J Paul Getty

All experience is an arch, to build upon.

Henry Adams

The lure of the distant and the difficult is deceptive. The great opportunity is where you are.

John Burroughs

People are ambitious and unrealistic. They set targets for themselves that are higher than what you would set them. And because they set them, they hit them.

Liisa Joronen

The ability to accept responsibility is the measure of the man.

Roy L Smith

Advertisements contain the only truths
to be relied on in a newspaper.
Thomas Jefferson

Creativity is allowing oneself to make mistakes.
Art is knowing which ones to keep.
William Adams

Dreams have their place in management activity, but they need to be kept severely under control.

Sir Arnold Weinstock

Take care of those who work for you and you'll float to greatness on their achievements.

H S M Burns

The difference between a leader and a boss is the difference between good and bad management.

Joe Klock

If you can't smell it, you can't sell it.

Estée Lauder

There are three kinds of lies: lies, damned lies, and statistics.

Benjamin Disraeli

When you marry your mistress, you create a job vacancy.

Sir James Goldsmith

A primitive artist is an amateur whose work sells.

Grandma Moses

If a man runs after money, he's money-mad; if he keeps it, he's a capitalist; if he spends it he's a playboy; if he doesn't get it, he's a ne'er-do-well; if he doesn't try to get it, he lacks ambition. If he gets it without working for it, he's a parasite; and if he accumulates it after a lifetime of hard work, people call him a fool who never got anything out of life.

Vic Oliver

That's the American way. If little kids don't aspire to make money like I did, what the hell good is this country?

Lee Iacocca

Your company does not belong in any market where it cannot be the best.

Philip Kotler

More strategies fail because they are overripe than because they are premature.

Kenichi Ohmae

People find gold in fields, veins, river beds and pockets. Whichever, it takes work to get it out.

Art Linkletter

My father said:'You must never try to make all the money that's in a deal. Let the other fellow make some money too, because if you have a reputation for always making all the money … you won't make many deals.'

J Paul Getty

If you have to support yourself, you had bloody well better find some way that is going to be interesting.

Katharine Hepburn

Never invest your money in anything that eats or needs repainting. Billy Rose

Always take a job that is too big for you.

Harry Emerson Fosdick

Written instructions are seldom adequate and personal involvement is essential.

David Packard

All bad precedents began as justifiable measures.

Julius Caesar

Information about money has become almost as important as money itself ... The guy with the competitive advantage is the one with the best technology.

Walter Wriston

Growth does not always lead a business to build on success. All too often it converts a highly successful business into a mediocre large business.

Richard Branson

Fireflies throwing off sparks before the storm.

Lou Gerstner (describing 'dot.com' companies)

How can they say my life isn't a success? Have I not for more than sixty years got enough to eat and escaped being eaten?

Logan Pearsall Smith

My number one job here at Apple is to make sure that the top one hundred people are A+ players. And everything else will take care of itself.

Steve Jobs

The brain is a wonderful organ. It starts working the moment you get up in the morning, and does not stop until you get into the office.

Robert Frost

A decision is an action an executive must take when he has information so incomplete that the answer does not present itself.

Arthur William Radford

I don't invest in anything I don't
understand – it makes more sense
to buy TV stations than oil wells.
Oprah Winfrey

**Trust comes back to the character,
behaviour, and values of the company. You
only achieve trust and retain it if you
behave in a way which inspires trust.**
Dominic Cadbury

I look for those sharp, scratchy, harsh,
almost unpleasant guys who see and tell
you about things as they really are.
Thomas J Watson Jnr

Success can be achieved
only through repeated
failure and introspection.
In fact, success represents
1 per cent of your work
which results only from
the 99 per cent that is
called failure.

Soichiro Honda

There are but two means of locomotion to the top. Either people must like you so much that they push you there, or you, yourself, are so good that you push yourself there.

Gerald Sparrow

The illiterate of the year 2000 will not be the individual who cannot read and write, but the one who cannot learn, unlearn, and relearn.

Alvin Toffler

In a sense, every business today, not just the garment trade, is a 'fashion' business. To compete effectively, companies must innovate continually and in ever shorter cycles.

Rosabeth Moss Kanter

I have learned the novice can often see things that the expert overlooks.

Tom Peters

To suppose, as we all suppose, that we could be rich and not behave as the rich behave, is like supposing that we could drink all day and keep absolutely sober.

Logan Pearsall Smith

To me, it's very simple; if you're going to be thinking anyway, you might as well think big. Donald Trump

Samuel Butler

The money that men make lives after them.

Greed is all right … Greed is healthy. You can be greedy and still feel good about yourself.

Ivan Boesky

A man is not idle because he is absorbed in thought. There is a visible labour and there is an invisible labour.

Victor Hugo

Men always try to keep women out of business so they won't find out how much fun it really is.

Vivien Kellems

Don't worry about people stealing an idea. If it's original, you will have to ram it down their throats.

Howard Aiken

A problem well stated is a problem half solved.

Charles F Kettering

Being good in business is the most fascinating kind of art.

Andy Warhol

I indispensably contributed to saving Eastern Europe.

Robert Maxwell

If you can keep your head when all about you are losing theirs, it's just possible you haven't grasped the situation.
Jean Kerr

Anyone who attempts anything original in the world must expect a bit of ridicule.
Alberto Jauntorena

The chief weakness in business organisation is lack of coordination.

Mary Parker Follett

In business we cut each others' throats, but now and then we sit around the same table and behave – for the sake of the ladies.

Aristotle Onassis

Innovation is the specific instrument of entrepreneurship.

Peter F Drucker

Money can't buy friends, but you get a better class of enemy.

Spike Milligan

Capital as such is not evil; it is its wrong use that is evil.

Mohandas Gandhi

Japan took its success for granted. Now it does not really want to face, does not know how to face, the empty charade of subsidy and protection.

Kenichi Ohmae

The salary of the chief executive of the large corporation is not a market award for achievement. It is frequently in the nature of a warm personal gesture by the individual to himself.

J K Galbraith

When you reach for the stars, you may not quite get one, but you won't come up with a handful of mud either.

Leo Burnett

We don't know how to sell products based on performance. Everything we sell, we sell based on image.

Roberto Goizueta

The goal of a big business person should be to create a new organisation that feels and operates like a smaller business.

John P Kotter

All our talents increase in the using, and every faculty, both good and bad, strengthens by exercise.

Anne Brontë

If you do it right fifty-one percent of the time you will end up a hero.

Alfred P Sloan

Do not lose yourself in the work.

Sri Aurobindo

The true role of advertising is exactly that of the first salesman hired by the first manufacturer – to get business away from his competitors.

Rosser Reeves

She was 'honeychile' in New Orleans,
The hottest of the bunch;
But on the old expense account,
She was gas, cigars and lunch.

Anonymous

There's no business without show business.

Michael J Wolf

Money is what you'd get on beautifully without if only other people weren't so crazy about it.
Margaret Case Harriman

Anyone who thinks there's safety in numbers hasn't looked at the stock market pages.
Irene Peter

Honesty is for the most part less profitable than dishonesty.

Plato

Business is a game, the greatest game in the world if you know how to play it.

Thomas J Watson Snr

The consumer is the most important part of the production line.

W Edwards Deming

Nothing succeeds like
the appearance of success.

Christopher Lasch

Do not delegate an assignment and then attempt to manage it yourself.

Wess Roberts

Executives are like joggers.
If you stop a jogger, he goes
on running on the spot.
If you drag an executive
away from his business,
he goes on running on the
spot, pawing the ground,
talking business.

Jean Baudrillard

Proficient is defined with one word: skilled. In order to become skilled you must have more than knowledge, you need to apply that information.

Jac Fitz-Enz

Experience teaches you that the man who looks you straight in the eye, particularly if he adds a firm handshake, is hiding something.

Clifton Fadiman

It is sobering to reflect on the extent to which the structure of our business has been dictated by the limitations of the file folder.

Michael Hammer

The fellow who never makes a mistake
takes his orders from one who does.
Herbert V Prochnow

If you don't want prosperity to falter, then Buy, Buy, Buy – on credit, of course. In other words, the surest way of bringing on a rainy day is to prepare for it.
Joseph Wood Krutch

It's possible to own too much. A man with one watch knows what time it is; a man with two watches is never quite sure.
Lee Segal

Due to the present financial situation, the light at the end of the tunnel will be turned off at the weekends.

Graffito

We do not make something because the demand, the market, is there. With our technology we can create demand, we can create the market. Supply creates its own demand.

Soichiro Honda

To improve the golden moment of opportunity, and catch the good that is within our reach, is the great art of life.

Samuel Johnson

We haven't got the money, so we've got to think. Ernest Rutherford

It's better to be a pirate than join the Navy.

Steve Jobs

Life's a continuous business, and so is success, and requires continuous effort.

Lady Thatcher

I'm not going to rest until we're shipping cars to Japan.

H Ross Perot

What's the most important thing you can tell me about leadership? I'd say, 'Just treat people the way you'd want to be treated.'

H Ross Perot

The single most dangerous word to be spoken in business is 'no'. The second most dangerous word is 'yes'. It is possible to avoid saying either.

Lois Wyse

The great enemy of clear language is insincerity.

George Orwell

Those who invented the law of supply and demand have no right to complain when this law works against their interest.

Anwar Sadat

The first steps to becoming a really great manager are simply common sense; but common sense is not very common.

Gerald M Blair

By observing California's youngsters on roller skates, a Sony engineer came up with the concept of the Walkman.

Kenichi Ohmae

I look forward to the day when we don't think in terms of a woman executive at all, but just an executive.

Ellen Gordon

Procrastination – the art of
keeping up with yesterday.
Don Marquis

Performance stands out like a ton
of diamonds. Nonperformance can
always be explained away.
Harold S Geneen

No sensible decision can be made without
taking into account not only the world as
it is, but the world as it will be.
Isaac Asimov

Dispatch is the soul of business, and nothing contributes more to Dispatch than Method.

Lord Chesterfield

Don't be afraid to be unique or speak your mind because that's what makes you different from everyone else.

Dave Thomas

You know the saying, 'A horse always knows when the rider is afraid'? That is true of business as well.

Dennis Stevenson

Since business is a 'get things done' institution, creativity without action-oriented follow-through is a barren form of behaviour.

Theodore Levitt

It has been said that the love of money is the root of all evil. The want of money is so quite as truly.

Samuel Butler

If you don't say anything you won't be called on to repeat it.

Calvin Coolidge

Retired is being tired twice, I've thought,
First tired of working,
Then tired of not.

Richard Armour

Advertising isn't a science. It's persuasion. And persuasion is an art.

Bill Bernbach

The great enemy of clear language is insincerity.

George Orwell

The information highway will transform our culture as dramatically as Gutenberg's press did in the Middle Ages.

Bill Gates

Oil-price forecasters
make sheep seem like
independent thinkers.

Michael C Lynch

Leadership is not about being
nice. It's about being right
and being strong.

Paul Keating

If I needed a banker,
I would go to me. No one
really does what I do.

Nancy Peretsman

The engine that drives enterprise is not thrift but profit.

John Maynard Keynes

Drudgery, calamity, exasperation, want, are instructors in eloquence and wisdom.

Ralph Waldo Emerson

Stretch and discipline are the yin and yang of business.

Christopher Bartlett

You can't expect a viable economy if the only object of government policy is to be re-elected every four years.
Sir Arnold Weinstock

To be vital, an organisation has to repot itself, start again, get new ideas, renew itself.
Jack Welch

When I was young I thought that money was the most important thing in life; now that I am old I know it is.

Oscar Wilde

Customers are your future, representing new opportunities, ideas and avenues for growth.

Michael Dell

Whatever the business model, it doesn't matter what anybody else thinks if customers don't like it.

Paul Gratton

Life without industry is guilt, industry without art is brutality.

John Ruskin

In God we trust, everyone else must pay cash.

Anonymous

Managerial intellect wilted in competition with managerial adrenaline. The thrill of the chase blinded pursuers to the consequences of the chase.

Warren Buffett

Women's presence in the office work force challenged the Victorian
ideal of separate public and private worlds for men and women.

Angela Kwolek-Folland

Everything that is properly
business we must keep carefully
separate from *life*. Business
requires earnestness and method;
life must have a freer handling.

Goethe

True, you can't take it with you,
but then, that's not the place
where it comes in handy.

Brendan Francis

Next to being shot at and missed,
nothing is quite as satisfying as
an income tax refund.

F J Raymond

So much of what we call
management consists in making
it difficult for people to work.

Peter Drucker

The first rule of intelligent tinkering is to save all the parts.

Paul Ehrlich

Self-made men are very apt to usurp the prerogative of the Almighty and overwork themselves.

Edgar Wilson Nye

The man who starts out simply with the idea of getting rich won't succeed, you must have a larger ambition.

John D Rockefeller

Leaders are the most result-oriented individuals in the world.

Warren Bennis

A memorandum is written not to inform the reader but to protect the writer.
Dean Acheson

Every great man of business has got somewhere a touch of the idealist in him.
Woodrow Wilson

It is not the crook in modern business that we fear, but the honest man who does not know what he is doing.

Owen D Young

The dynamics of capitalism is postponement of enjoyment to the constantly postponed future.

Norman O Brown

The music industry is toast. It has been completely overtaken by events and can do nothing about it.

Shaun Fanning

Miracles can be made, but only by sweating.

Giovanni Agnelli

Trahey's Simple Rule: Would you hire you?

Jane Trahey

Nothing in the world can take the place of persistence.

Ray Kroc

What is robbing a bank compared with founding a bank?

Bertolt Brecht

It is not that pearls fetch a high price *because* men have dived for them; but on the contrary, men have dived for them because they fetch a high price.

Richard Whately

Unless a man has been taught what to do with success after getting it, the achievement of it must inevitably leave him a prey to boredom.

Bertrand Russell

He that resolves to deal only with honest men must leave off dealing.

Thomas Fuller

In the global economy the challenges and changes are universal.

Robert Heller

The driving force for the development of new products is not technology, not money, but the imagination of people.

David Packard

If one advances confidently in the direction of his dreams, and endeavours to live the life that he has imagined, he will meet with a success unexpected in common hours.

Henry David Thoreau

Prosperity is only an instrument to be used, not a deity to be worshipped.

Calvin Coolidge

Often the most effective facilitators in learning processes are not professional trainers but the line managers themselves. Peter Senge

Economy: cutting down other people's wages. J B Morton

The trouble with the rat race is that even if you win, you're still a rat.

Lily Tomlin

The consumer is not a moron. She is *your wife*. And she is grown up.

David Ogilvy

I believe in the dignity of labour, whether with head or hand; that the world owes every man an opportunity to make a living.

John D Rockefeller Jr

If the washroom isn't good enough for the people in charge, then it's not good enough for the people in the store.

Lord Sieff

Over the past twenty-five years, economic forecasters have missed four of the past five recessions.

Business Week (1996)

At Amstrad the staff start early and finish late ... It's all action and the atmosphere is amazing, and the *esprit de corps* is terrific. Working hard is fun.

Alan Sugar

The moment you let avoiding failure become your motivator, you're down the path of inactivity.

Roberto Goizueta

Perfect freedom is reserved for the man who lives by his own work and, in that work, does what he wants to do.

R G Collingwood

The person who knows 'how' will always have a job. The person who knows 'why' will always be his boss.

Diane Ravitch

I liked the shaver so much I bought the
company [Remington Corporation]
Victor Kiam

There are three kinds of economist.
Those who can count and those who can't.
Eddie George

There is no future in any job. The future
lies in the man who holds the job.
Dr George Crane

People who are successful simply want
it more than people who are not.
Ian Schrager

To be always ready a man must be able to cut a knot, for everything cannot be untied.

Henri Frédéric Amiel

It's not just running a restaurant, it's being friends with your customers. It's a personal connection.

Mary Kelekis

The money coming into the game [football] is incredible. But it is just the prune-juice effect – it comes in and goes out straight away. Agents run the game.

Alan Sugar

Ultimately, the job of the manager is to get ordinary people to create extraordinary results.

Christopher Bartlett

In a hierarchy every employee tends to rise to his level of incompetence.

Laurence J Peter

There's a certain really quite unimaginable intellectual interest that one gets from working in the context where you have to put broad theoretical and fairly complex conceptual issues to the test in the market place.

Alan Greenspan

People assume you slept your way to the top. Frankly, I couldn't sleep my way to the middle. Joni Evans

John Gall

Systems tend to grow, and as they grow, they encroach.

The only thing that hurts more than paying an income tax is not having to pay an income tax.

Lord Dewar

Taxes are a barrier to progress, and they punish rather than reward success.

Steve Forbes

If all economists were laid end to end, they would not reach a conclusion.

George Bernard Shaw

I felt the only way to turn things round was to get people to think like owners.

Jack Stack

Immature artists imitate. Mature artists steal.

Lionel Trilling

For me coming second is the same as coming last.

Lord Grade

> Thou, O God, dost sell us all good things at the price of labour.

Leonardo da Vinci

We're facing a danger that economics is rigorous deduction based upon faulty assumptions.

W Brian Arthur

We're drowning in information and starving for knowledge.

Rutherford D Rogers

Don't hurry, don't worry.
You're here for a short visit. So be
sure to stop and smell the flowers.

Walter Hagen

We need a can-do, vibrant,
innovation-driven culture. Not
wearing a tie is just a snippet of that.

Paul Walsh

Never take a reference from a
clergyman. They always want to
give someone a second chance.

Lady Selborne

If we're going to run this business [IBM] on viscera, it's going to be my viscera.

Thomas J Watson Jr

We may convince others by our arguments; but we can only persuade them by their own.

Joseph Joubert

Money never remains just coins and pieces of paper. Money can be translated into the beauty of living, a support in misfortune, an education, a future security. It can also be translated into a source of bitterness.

Sylvia Porter

There is no reason to be the richest man in the cemetery. You can't do any business from there.

Colonel Sanders

If advertisers spent the same amount of money on improving their products as they do on advertising then they wouldn't have to advertise them.

Will Rogers

Revitalising General Motors was like teaching an elephant to tap dance. You find the sensitive spot and start poking.

H Ross Perot

A good manager is a man who isn't worried about his own career but rather the careers of those who work for him.

H S M Burns

Too bad that all the people who know how to run the country are busy driving taxicabs and cutting hair.

George Burns

Promise, large promise, is the soul of an advertisement.

Samuel Johnson

The buyer needs a hundred eyes, the seller not one.

George Herbert

There are four things that hold back human progress. Ignorance, stupidity, committees and accountants.

Sir Charles James Lyall

Our wages are lower, our holidays are shorter, our working hours are longer – simply because we produce less per man employed.

Michael Clapham

The only question with wealth is what you do with it.

John D Rockefeller Jr

What did it for me? It wasn't my education or experience. It was my passion.

Andrea Jung

The role of management is always to identify the weakest links, support them and strengthen them.

Ron Dennis

Any argument worth making within the bureaucracy must be capable of being expressed in a simple declarative sentence that is obviously true once stated.

John McNaughton

There is only one boss. The customer. And he can fire everybody in the company, from the chairman on down, simply by spending his money somewhere else.

Sam Walton

There are plenty of recommendations on how to get out of trouble cheaply and fast. Most of them come down to the same thing. Deny your responsibility.

Nancy Peretsman

Put not your trust in money,
but put your money in trust.

Oliver Wendell Holmes Sr

There's only room for one bigmouth in my organisation, and that's me.

Alan Sugar

Vision: Top management's heroic guess about the future, easily printed on mugs, T-shirts, posters, and calendar cards.

Anonymous

Science, engineering and technology are fundamental drivers in the economy of the future, providing the foundation for business growth and overall improvement in the quality of life.

Mark Birrell

The task of industry is continuously, year on year, to make more and better things, using less of the world's resources.

Sir John Harvey-Jones

If you have enough meetings over a long enough period of time, the meetings become more important than the problem that the meetings were intended to solve.

E R Hendrickson

I feel these days like a very large flamingo. No matter which way I turn, there is always a very large bill.
Joseph O'Connor

Men, like nails, lose their usefulness when they lose direction and begin to bend.
Walter Savage Landor

Men don't have some special genetic coding that makes them better fit for playing the markets. It's simply a matter of education and knowledge.
Sue Herera

A negative judgement gives you more satisfaction than praise, providing it smacks of jealousy.

Jean Baudrillard

If you don't do it excellently, don't do it at all. Because if it's not excellent, it won't be profitable or fun, and if you're not in business for fun or profit, what the hell are you doing there?

Robert Townsend

After all is said and done, a hell of a lot more is said than done.

Clark Omstead

A diplomat is a person who can tell you to go to hell in such a way that you actually look forward to the trip. Caskie Stinnett

Define your business goals clearly so that others can see them as you do.

George Burns

The big danger in mega-mergers is that they are seen as a mating of dinosaurs.

Peter Bonfield

Not to decide
is to decide.

Harvey Cox

New money does more to determine good performance than good performance does to attract new money.

Alan Pope

There are only two things to aim at in life: first, to get what you want; and, after that, to enjoy it. Only the wisest of mankind achieve the second.

Logan Pearsall Smith

Quality is characteristic of a product or service that helps somebody and which has a market.

W Edwards Deming

We listen to what our employees want and it shows up in everything from the layout of our offices to the benefits and amenities.

Raul Fernandez

Good times, bad times, there will always be advertising. In good times people want to advertise; in bad times they have to.

Bruce Barton

Make a suggestion or assumption and let them tell you you're wrong. People also have a need to feel smarter than you are.

Mark McCormack

Xerox: a trademark for a photocopying device that can make rapid reproductions of human error, perfectly.

Merle L Meacham

A lot of people who complain about
their boss being stupid would be out
of a job if he were any smarter.
Chuck Combs

Did you ever expect a corporation to have
a conscience, when it has no soul to be
damned, and no body to be kicked?
Lord Edward Thurlow

When business is good it pays to have
public relations; when business is bad
you've got to have public relations.
Anonymous

Develop the
business around
the people; build it,
don't buy it; and,
then, be the best.

Richard Branson

Whoever is first in the field and awaits the coming of the enemy, will be fresh for the fight; whoever is second in the field and has to hasten to battle will arrive exhausted.

Sun Tzu

It might be said that it is the ideal of the employer to have production without employees and the ideal of the employee is to have income without work.

E F Schumacher

Globalisation requires that organisations adopt a cross-cultural perspective to be successful in accomplishing their goals in the context of a global economy.

Rabi S Bhagat

The learning person looks forward to failure or mistakes.

Warren Bennis

Changes are not without cost. They produce reactionaries that fight to block progress. We have found it possible to minimize resistance by establishing a culture based on core values.

Charles G Koch

Total commercial honesty always costs something, but total or partial dishonesty will cost more. Robert Heller

Albert Einstein

Imagination is more important than knowledge.

The function of the expert is not to be more right than other people, but to be wrong for more sophisticated reasons.

David Butler

The history of Scotland
is one of theology
tempered by homicide.

Ivor Brown

Many a man's reputation
would not know his character
if they met on the street.

Elbert Hubbard

I don't know anything
about music. In my line,
you don't have to.

Elvis Presley

If I see something I like, I buy it;

then I try to sell it.

Lord Grade

I don't think too many people would want my job. I'm a bit of a nutter.

Alan Sugar

If you drop something and it doesn't break, mark it heavy duty.

Mitch Hellman

Optimism tends to expand to fill the scope available for its exercise.
Edward Merrow

Clothes don't make the man – but they go a long way towards making a businessman.
Thomas J Watson Sr

Nothing will ever be attempted,
if all possible objections must
first be overcome.

Samuel Johnson

The rule is, jam tomorrow and jam
yesterday – but never jam today.

Lewis Carroll

Take our twenty best people away,
and I tell you that Microsoft would
become an unimportant company.

Bill Gates

A good goal is like a strenuous exercise – it makes you stretch.

Mary Kay Ash

Say nothing of my debts unless you mean to pay them.

English Proverb

The real essence of work is concentrated energy … people who have that in a superior degree … are independent of the forms, habits and artifices by which … less active people are kept in their labours.

Walter Bagehot

If you're not happy with yourself, how can you make the customer happy?

Liisa Joronen

Bonuses, as well as salaries, reward the finding and sharing of ideas even more than their origination.

Jack Welch

The god of the cannibals will be a cannibal, of the crusaders a crusader, and of the merchants a merchant.

Ralph Waldo Emerson

The effort expended by a bureaucracy in defending any error is in direct proportion to the size of the error.

John Nies

A leader is a man who has the ability to get other people to do what they don't want to do and like it.

Harry S Truman

The public be damned! I'm working for my stockholders.

William H Vanderbilt

It's the economy, stupid.

Bill Clinton

Luck is not chance –
It's Toil –
Fortune's expensive smile
Is earned –

Emily Dickinson

It's a very sobering feeling to be up in space and realize that one's safety factor was determined by the lowest bidder on a government contract.

Alan Shepherd

When it comes to mergers, hope triumphs over experience.

Irwin Stelzer

Opportunities are usually disguised as hard work, so most people don't recognise them.
Ann Landers

To be mission-based means that those in positions of authority are not the source of authority.
Peter Senge

Live within your income, even if you have to borrow to do so.

Josh Billings

Sometimes by losing a battle you find a new way to win the war.

Donald Trump

There are two kinds of statistics, the kind you look up and the kind you make up.

Rex Stout

There is no royal flower-strewn path to success.

C J Walker

Criticism is one of the most important tasks a manager has.

Daniel Goleman

We always admire the other fellow more after we have tried his job.

William Feather

A mediocre idea that generates enthusiasm will go further than a great idea that inspires no one.

Mary Kay Ash

The largest profits go to those businesses which most devotedly follow a policy of insisting on a competitive advantage, no matter how small, for every product or service they market.

R H Beeby

Anybody who runs a successful high tech
company has to be an eternal optimist;
has to be able to take big risks.

John Sculley

Everything changes when there is
a real customer yelling at you from
the other end of the phone.

Percy Barnevik

When you are skinning your customers,
you should leave some skin on to grow
so that you can skin them again.

Nikita Khrushchev

Financial capital is better situated in the global system than industrial capital; once a plant has been built, moving it is difficult.

George Soros

I've spent thirty years going round factories. When you know something's wrong, nine times out of ten it's the management … people aren't being led right. And bad leaders invariably blame the people.

John Harvey-Jones

Lethargy bordering on sloth remains the cornerstone of our investment style.

Warren Buffett

Management consultants … are people who borrow your watch to tell you what time it is and then walk off with it. Robert Townsend

Don't try to think like the top until you are the top.

David Ormerod

The gambling known as business looks with austere disfavour upon the business known as gambling.

Ambrose Bierce

All costs walk on two legs.

Arjay Miller

The kind of brain-dead, gum chewing assistant you find in so many shops drives me wild. I want everyone who works for me to feel the same excitement I feel.

Anita Roddick

In the business world an executive knows something about everything, a technician knows everything about something and the switchboard operator knows everything.

Harold Coffin

There are some extremely sharp investment advisors who can get you in at the bottom of the market. There are some extremely sharp investment advisors who can get you out at the top. They are never the same people.

Gary North

Again and again in business history, an unknown competitor comes from nowhere and in a few short years overtakes the established leaders without apparently even breathing hard.

Peter Drucker

You've got to figure out a way to manage the complexity of large projects yet still allow your core teams to focus on the essentials.

Steve Jobs

Focus Groups are people who are selected on the basis of their inexplicable free time and their common love of free sandwiches.

Scott Adams

We live in an economy where knowledge, not buildings and machinery, is the chief resource and where knowledge-workers make up the biggest part of the work force.

Peter Drucker

Making a success of the job in hand is the
best step toward the kind you want.
Bernard Baruch

I hope we shall crush in its birth the
aristocracy of our monied corporations
which dare already to challenge our
government to a trial of strength, and bid
defiance to the laws of our country.
Thomas Jefferson

The people who have something to say
don't talk, the others insist on talking.
A J Liebling

A molehill man is a psuedo-busy executive who comes to work at 9 am and finds a molehill on his desk. He has until 5 pm to make this molehill into a mountain.

Fred Allen

When you meet someone better than yourself, turn your thoughts to becoming his equal. When you meet someone not as good as you are, look within and examine your own self.

Confucius

The contribution which the human mind makes to work and business is very much one of picking up information from tiny, seemingly insignificant trifles, and relating them to new ideas or concepts.

Sir John Harvey-Jones

Leaders who understand their organisations can articulate the negatives as well as the positives of their organisations.

Jay R Galbraith

There are in business three things necessary – knowledge, temper and time.

Owen Feltham

Top executives know that they have to shift to a talent-based, flat structure, but don't know what to do with all the entitled, middle-aged managers they have.

Yashuhiro Fukushima

Guidelines for bureaucrats: (1) When in charge, ponder. (2) When in trouble, delegate. (3) When in doubt, mumble. James H Boren

James L Davis

In business, price increases as service declines.

Intellectual capital is the sum of everything everybody in a company knows that gives it a competitive edge.

Thomas A Stewart

Automation does not make optimism obsolete.

Keith Funston

Effective visions are lived in details, not broad strokes.

Tom Peters

Nothing is more terrible than activity without insight.

Thomas Carlyle

I've written books on advertising …

cheque books.

Alan Sugar

Work seven days a week and nothing can stop you.

John Moores

> # Sometimes your best investments are the ones you don't make.

Donald Trump

A government which robs Peter to pay Paul
can always depend on the support of Paul.
George Bernard Shaw

Good executives never put off until tomorrow
what they can get someone else to do today.
Dr John C Maxwell

We don't manage people here [at Goretex]. People manage themselves.

Wilbert Lee Gore

Whoever I pick as my apprentice, has gotta fit in at my company.

Alan Sugar

A common mistake about the image of a manager is that they must be loud, flamboyant, and a great drinker … This is wrong.

Gerald M Blair

In the affluent society, no useful distinction can be made between luxuries and necessities.

J K Galbraith

The web site needs to be as sticky as a currant bun.

Carolyn McCall

Hoarding information or getting it first was one way managers in traditional companies expressed their power. But information blockages make the whole system less effective.

Rosabeth Moss Kanter

Orange was never just another mobile phone company. It was a promise delivered.

Hans Snook

The bottom line that determines success for either a man or a woman is: 'Can you make money?' That, in essence, makes gender less relevant.

Bernadette Murphy

A road that does not lead to other roads always has to be retraced, unless the traveller chooses to rust at the end of it.

Tehyi Hsieh

Destiny is not a matter of chance, it is a matter of choice; it is not a thing to be waited for, it is a thing to be achieved.

William Jennings Bryan

A handful of men have become very rich by paying attention to details that most others ignored.

Henry Ford

With credit, you can buy everything you can't afford.

Edith Bunker

What you get free costs too much.

Jean Anouilhs

Managing a business requires a great deal of frankness and openness and you actually lead by being very honest with people.

Michael Edwardes

The genius of a good leader is to leave behind him a situation which common sense, without the grace of genius, can deal with successfully.

Walter Lippmann

Learning is not compulsory, neither is survival.

Peter Zwack

When the effective leader is finished with his work, the people say it happened naturally.
Laozi

Business is often about killing your favourite children to allow others to succeed.
Sir John Harvey-Jones

I'm very sympathetic to the view that the economy should spend more time in dealing with the predicament of people who are thrown into turmoil when things go wrong.

Amartya Sen

Technology is dominated by two types of people: those who understand what they do not manage, and those who manage what they do not understand.

Archibald Putt

There is no shortage of creative people in American business. The shortage is of innovators. All too often people believe that creativity leads to innovation. It doesn't.

Theodore Levitt

Live out of your imagination, not your history.

Arthur Bryan

Creativity can be described as letting go of certainties.

Gail Sheehy

Forty percent of businesses will be owned by women. Women are saying, 'I don't belong in this company. I'm sick of fighting this battle.'

Faith Popcorn

Surround yourself with the best people you can find, delegate authority and don't interfere.

Ronald Reagan

We can no longer draw a line around business and say that is not our problem. If it is a problem for society, it is our problem also. The question is not whether it is our problem, but what our capacity and legitimacy is as a business to contribute a solution.

Mark Moody-Stuart

Business is many things, the least of which is the balance sheet. It is a fluid, ever changing, living thing, sometimes building to great peaks, sometimes falling to crumpled lumps.

Harold S Green

Corporation: An ingenious device
for obtaining profit without
individual responsibility.
Ambrose Bierce

It's a vibrant special place, it really
is like being in Italy during
the Renaissance.
Donna Dubinsky (describing Silicon Valley)

Never put off till tomorrow what you
can do the day after tomorrow.
Mark Twain

The truth is if you don't say you can do a job, someone else in the world will, and you'll be left behind.

Richard D'Aveni

Although strategic planning is billed as a way of becoming more future oriented, most managers … will admit that their strategic plans reveal more about today's problems than tomorrow's opportunities.

Gary Hamel

The challenge in a start-up is that you have to spread your wings pretty far to see what will work.

Michael Dell

Once you decide to work for yourself, you never go back to work for somebody else. Alan Sugar

If you can't convince them, confuse them.

Harry S Truman

Private enterprise is the power ... state control is the machine.

Stephen Leacock

The bill was due before you got it.

John Shelton

Remember that on day one, when you go in as the boss, you'll feel a mixture of exhilaration that you've made it and fatigue with all the effort.

Barbara Thomas

I would advise young companies, particularly the small dot.com companies, to pay close attention to their service levels.

Lillian Vernon

Mr Morgan [J Pierpont Morgan, banker] buys his partners; I grow my own.

Andrew Carnegie

Whenever you're sitting across from some important person, always picture him sitting there in a suit of long red underwear. That's the way I always operated in business.

Jospeh P Kennedy

Consultants eventually leave, which makes them excellent scapegoats for major management blunders.

Scott Adams

The highest art of professional management requires the literal ability to smell a real fact from all others.

Harold S Geneen

I always thought if you worked hard enough and tried hard enough, things would work out. I was wrong.

Katherine Graham

If women didn't exist, all the money in the world would have no meaning.
Aristotle Onassis

To mistake money for wealth, is the same sort of error as to mistake the highway which may be the easiest way of getting to your house or lands, for the house and lands themselves.
John Stuart Mill

To turn $100 into $110 is work. To turn $100 million into $110 million is inevitable.
Edgar Bronfman

Wealth – any income that is at least one hundred dollars more a year than the income of one's wife's sister's husband.

H L Mencken

We don't so much have a marketing department, as anthropologists working for us.

Anita Roddick

Discrimination is the capacity to discern what is important.

Warren Blank

If you run one business well, you can run any business well.

Richard Branson

Saving is a very fine thing, especially when your parents have done it for you.

Winston Churchill

It has long been an axiom of mine that the little things are infinitely the most important.

Arthur Conan Doyle

I've done things that everybody said couldn't be done, and I've done them in what everybody said was a crazy way. If any young man comes to me and asks how to make his fortune, I tell him to do the same. Don't follow everybody else. Get off the beaten track. Be a little mad.

Jeno Paulucci

In this world there are only two tragedies. One is not getting what one wants, and the other is getting it.
Oscar Wilde

Richard C Smolik

Anything highly publicised needs to be.

Truth is the glue that holds governments together. Compromise is the oil that makes governments go.

Karl Augustus Menninger

Once a decision was made, I did not worry about it afterwards.

Harry S Truman

Some people grow with responsibility – others merely swell.

Abram Sachar

If you don't know where you are going, any road will get you there.

John Hildebrandt

First get in, then get rich, then get respectable.

Bernie Eccleston

Success is the one unpardonable sin against one's fellows.

Ambrose Bierce

> # The growth of a large business is merely the survival of the fittest.

John D Rockefeller

Security no longer comes from being employed. It comes from being employable.
Rosabeth Moss Kanter

The usefulness of a meeting is in inverse proportion to the attendance.
Lane Kirkland

I can tell more about how someone is likely to react in a business situation from one round of golf than I can from a hundred hours of meetings.
Mark McCormack

The essential functions of the executives are first to provide the system of communication, second to promote the securing of essential efforts and, third, to formulate and define purpose.
Chester Barnard

The test of a vocation is the love of the drudgery it involves.

Logan Pearsall Smith

Never sing in chorus if you want to be heard.

Jules Archibald

The core corporation is … increasingly a façade, behind which teems an array of decentralized groups and subgroups continuously contracting with similarly diffuse working units all over the world.

Robert Reich

One cannot walk through a mass-production factory and not feel that one is in hell.

W H Auden

It's important to understand that investing is in no way an intellectual pursuit in which 'research', 'information', and 'business degrees' are more important than common sense, greed control, discipline, and experience.

Steven R Selengut

In the foundation and development of a successful enterprise there must be a single-minded pursuit of financial profit.

C Northcote Parkinson

Competitive strategy is about being different. It means deliberately choosing a different set of activities to deliver a unique mix of values.

Michael Porter

For every failure, there's an alternative course of action. You just have to find it. When you come to a roadblock, take a detour.

Mary Kay Ash

Always do one thing less than you think you can do.

Bernard Baruch

Plan backward.

Joe Pangraze

A man may be concerned in the management of more than one business enterprise, but they should all be of the one kind, which he understands. The great successes of life are made by concentration.

Andrew Carnegie

I didn't fight to get women out from behind the vacuum cleaner to get them onto the board of Hoover.

Germaine Greer

Dollar making is not necessarily business.

Andrew Carnegie

A hospital should also have a recovery room adjoining the cashier's office.
Francis O'Walsh

What is actually happening is often less important that what appears to be happening.
William V Shannon

We all worry about the population explosion, but we don't worry about it at the right time.

Arthur Hoppe

By working faithfully eight hours a day, you may eventually get to be boss and work twelve hours a day.

Robert Frost

If a rich man is proud of his wealth, he should not be praised until it is known how he employs it.

Socrates

I must follow the people. Am I not their leader?

Benjamin Disraeli

When all think alike, no one thinks very much.

Walter Lippmann

The reason for the rush is the delay, and, conversely, the reason for the delay is the rush.

Lawrence Litt

In this world nothing is certain but death and taxes.

Benjamin Franklin

Nothing in the world can take the place of persistence. Talent will not; nothing is more common than unsuccessful men of talent. Genius will not; unrewarded genius is almost a proverb. Education will not; the world is full of educated derelicts. Persistence and determination are omnipotent.

Calvin Coolidge

When people are free to do
as they please, they usually
imitate each other.

Eric Hoffer

Make yourself necessary to someone.

Ralph Waldo Emerson

If you are a writer, editor, publisher,
or affiliated with an advertising
agency, everyone knows more about
your business than you do.

Jack Kneass

A business is only as good as the sum of its parts, which means you can't afford to have weak parts.

Robert Heller

Well-ventilated, well-lighted, and sanitarily kept workrooms, rest-rooms and other creature comforts provided in factories, stores, and office buildings are largely the results of women's presence in industry.

Edith Johnson

If the only tool you have is a hammer, you treat everything like a nail.

Abraham Maslow

Arguably the only goods people need these days are food and nappies. Sir Terence Conran

The only sure weapon against bad ideas is better ideas. **Whitney Griswold**

A verbal contract isn't worth the paper it's written on.

Sam Goldwyn

It's hard to find things that won't sell online.

Jeff Bezos

Your brightest, sharpest new employees are the first to leave your organisation – as the cream rises to the top it will be skimmed off.

Ken Rigsbee

A happy atmosphere is something that customers pick up on.

Tom Farmer

The whole thing is fire, ready, aim and I love it.

Chris Moore (describing 'dot.com' businesses)

My fundamental belief is that if a company wants to see the future, eighty percent of what it is going to have to learn will be from outside its own industry.

Gary Hamel

We are an indispensable team; *you* are overmanned; *they* are redundant.

Anthony Sampson

To last, a company must strive to add long-term value rather than going for the quick buck.

Charles G Koch

The new economy favours intangible things – ideas, information, and relationships.

Kevin Kelly

Every creative act is a sudden
cessation of stupidity.
Edwin Land

Everybody sets out to do something, and
everybody does something, but no one
does what he sets out to do.
George Moore

You can't learn too soon that the most
useful thing about a principle is that it can
always be sacrificed to expediency.
W. Somerset Maugham

The job for big companies, the challenge that we all face as bureaucrats, is to create an environment where people can reach their dreams – and they don't have to do it in a garage.

Jack Welch

If an idea is successful, the first person to claim credit for it will be the person who contended all along that it wouldn't work.

Norton Mockridge

The best careers advice given to the young is 'Find out what you like doing best and get someone to pay you for doing it.'

Katharine Whitehorn

We trained hard … but every time we were beginning to form up into teams, we would be reorganised. I was to learn later in life that we tend to meet any new situation by reorganising … a wonderful method it can be for creating the illusion of progress …

Petronius

Problems that go
away by themselves
come back by
themselves.

Marcy E David

There are no secrets to success: don't waste time
looking for them. Success is the result of perfection,
hard work, learning from failure, loyalty to those for
whom you work, and persistence.

Colin Powell

Women actually do quite well on Wall Street because
so much of this business is intuitive. Elizabeth MacKay

Andrew Jackson

One man with courage makes a majority.

[Leaders] are appreciators of talent and nurturers of talent and they have the ability to recognise valuable ideas.

Warren Bennis

The meek shall inherit the earth, but *not* the mineral rights.

J Paul Getty

The next best thing to knowing something is knowing where to find it.

Samuel Johnson

The sooner you fall behind, the more time you have to catch up.

Sam Ogden

I don't think I'm creative.

I think I recognise creativity.

Michael Grade

Music is spiritual, the music business is not.

Van Morrison

Price controls work best when they are needed least.

George P Shultz

Someone else probably has the same idea – so (a) get started, (b) plan to do it better.
Paul Obis

No one on his deathbed ever said, 'I wish I had spent more time on my business'.
Arnold Zack

It is ours to win with – if we can shift gears from decades of controlling things to a decade of liberty – turning people loose to dream, dare, and win.

Jack Welch

The basic philosophy of an organization has far more to do with its achievements than do technological or economic resources, organizational structure, innovation and timing.

Thomas J Watson

After hard work, the biggest determinant is being in the right place at the right time.

Michael Bloomberg

A thick skin is a gift from God.

Konrad Adenauer

The business of government is to keep the government out of business – that is, unless business needs government aid.

Will Rogers

The Internet will eventually converge with television. I have the relationships with entertainment companies and big technology companies to pull this off.

Geraldine Laybourne

Merchants have no country.

Thomas Jefferson

In the business world, everyone is paid in two coins: cash and experience. Take the experience first; the cash will come later.

Harold S Geneen

Stop competing on price; compete on value. Deliver total consumer solutions, rather than just your piece of the solution.

Faith Popcorn

If you hype something and it succeeds, you're a genius – it wasn't hype. If you hype it and it fails, then it's just a hype.

Neil Bogart

Economics limps along with one foot in untested hypotheses and the other in untestable slogans.

Joan Robinson

If you outsmart your lawyer, you've got the wrong lawyer.

John T Nolan

The test of any man lies in action.

Pindar

Creating value is an inherently cooperative process, capturing value is inherently competitive.

Barry J Nalebuff

The length of a meeting rises with the number of people present and the productiveness of a meeting falls with the square of the number of people present.

Eileen Shanahan

Success is that old ABC – ability, breaks and courage.

Charles Luckman

When you ask creative people how they did something, they feel a little guilty because they didn't really *do* it, they just *saw* something.
Steve Jobs

Where you stand depends on where you sit.
Rufus Miles

I don't think anybody yet has invented a pastime that's as much fun, or keeps you as young, as a good job.

Frederick Hudson Ecker

There are only two ways to get on in this world: by one's own industry, or by the weakness of others.

Jean de la Bruyère

Money won't buy happiness, but it will pay the salaries of a large research staff to study the problem.

Bill Vaughan

What the mind can believe, you can achieve.

Lorraine Moller

The reward of energy, enterprise and thrift – is taxes.

William Feather

The requirements for a successful Governor of the Bank of England are the tact and skill of an ambassador and the guile of a Romanian horse thief.

Harold Lever

Nothing is more central to any organisation's effectiveness than its ability to transmit accurate, relevant, understandable information among its members.

Saul W Gellerman

The Habitat philosophy has always been simple and unpretentious; we haven't made great statements … After all, the objects are good enough to speak for themselves and please in any environment.

Sir Terence Conran

You've got to let the monkey have the banana every once in a while.

Ed Laur

You should see some of the research
people. If they were in sales they'd never
get past the first base. Brilliant minds, but
no social graces whatsoever.
Elaine Garzarelli

Making money is fun, but it's pointless
if you don't use the power it brings.
John Bentley

I often thought that after you get
organised, you ought to throw
away the organisation chart.
David Packard

Companies, like people, cannot be skilful at everything. Therefore, core capabilities both advantage and disadvantage a company.

Dorothy Leonard

A lot of people think big business in America is a bad thing. I think it's a really good thing. Most people in business are ethical, hard-working, good people.

Steve Jobs

Anyone who says he isn't going to resign four times, definitely will.

J K Galbraith

The mass market has split into ever-multiplying, ever-changing sets of micromarkets that demand a continually expanding range of options. Alvin Toffler

Even in a hierarchy people can be equal as thinkers.

Nancy Kline

It is much easier to find a job than to keep one.

Jules Becker

Nothing fails
like success.

Ida B Mortford

The shortest and the best way to make your fortune is to let people see clearly that it is in their interests to promote yours.

Jean de la Bruyère

It is very vulgar to talk about one's own business. Only people like stockbrockers do that, and then merely at dinner parties.

Oscar Wilde

Give me fruitful error any time, full of seeds, bursting with its own corrections.

Vilfredo Pareto

It is at least conceivable that the twenty-first century business environment will be so fluid that it defies analysis, forcing executives to fall back upon hunch, or instinct.

John Elkington

In companies whose wealth is intellectual capital, networks, rather than hierarchies, are the right organisational design.

Thomas A Stewart

Connected individuals and their knowledge, not the corporation, are becoming the key organising unit.

Stan Davis

What makes me *feel* more successful than picking stocks or any of that, is my client relationships.

Grace Fey

Buy stocks like you buy groceries,
not like you buy your perfume.
Warren Buffett

Even though the leviathans have
remained rich and powerful, mass has
slowed them down and given openings
to the new and nimble.
Robert Heller

Political Economy or Economics
is a study of mankind in the
ordinary business of life.
Alfred Marshall

Good customers are an asset which, when well managed and served, will return a handsome lifetime income stream for the company.

Philip Kotler

Growth is like creativity, it doesn't go along very neat, precise plans. You get clogged highways before you figure out a way to open up capacity. You get pollution before you figure out a way to fight it.

Steve Forbes

It is possible for a business venture to be an island of efficiency in a sea of sloth.

Indira Gandhi

Job enrichment has been around for sixty years. It's been successful every time it has been tried, but industry is not interested.

Peter Drucker

Run with your head the first two thirds of a race and with your heart the final one third.

Jack Daniels

It used to be almost the first question (just after 'Can you type?') in the standard female job interview: 'Are you now, or have you ever, contemplated marriage, motherhood, or the violent overthrow of the US government?'

Barbara Ehrenreich

The most successful innovators are the creative imitators, the number two. Peter Drucker

Malcolm S Forbes

If you have a job without aggravations, you don't have a job.

Place a higher priority on discovering what a win looks like for the other person.

Harvey Robbins

It is tragic that Howard
Hughes had to die to
prove that he was alive.

Walter Kane

The less management knows
and understands, the more
secure the job.

Ivor Catt

Integrity is a lofty attitude
assumed by someone who
is unemployed.

Oscar Levant

People who fight fire with fire
usually end up with ashes.

Abigail Van Buren

The more opinions you have, the less you see.

Wim Wenders

Action will remove the doubt that theory cannot solve.

Tehyi Hsieh

Business without profit is not business any more than a pickle is a candy.
Charles F Abbot

The more complex a problem is, the more simple it is to resolve – in that more assumptions are available.
Ron Lindsey

You have to surround yourself
with people you trust, and people
that are good. But they also have
to be people who will tell the
emperor you have no clothes.

Oprah Winfrey

Good enough isn't good enough.

Paul W Steckel

If you can only cover costs,
capitalism is irrelevant.

Ernest F Cooke

Why should we be in such desperate haste to succeed, and in such desperate enterprises? If a man does not keep pace with his companions, perhaps it is because he hears a different drum.

Henry David Thoreau

My initial plan was to conquer the world, but in reality, the world is not that easy a place to conquer. I learned through the years that I had to build step by step, solidly.

Lise Watier

A life spent in making mistakes is not only more honourable but more useful than a life spent in doing nothing.

George Bernard Shaw

I always say to executives that they should go and see *King Lear*, because they'll be out there one day, wandering on the heath without a company car.

Charles Handy

Business is Darwinism – only the fittest survive.

Robert Holmes a'Court

It's not the hours you put in your work that count, it's work you put in your hours.

Sam Ewing

If you think you can win, you can win. Faith is necessary to victory.

William Hazlitt

Whenever you see a successful business, someone once made a courageous decision.

Peter Drucker

The desire for safety stands against every great and noble enterprise.

Tacitus

Economics is a subject that does not greatly respect one's wishes.

Nikita Khrushchev

Power corrupts, but lack of power corrupts absolutely.

Adlai Stevenson

The electronic highway is not merely open for business; it is relocating, restructuring, and literally redefining business in America.

Mary J Cronin

Many attempts to communicate are nullified by saying too much.

Robert Greenleaf

Stocks do not move unless they are pushed.

S Jay Levin

I gotta tell ya, you're fired!

Alan Sugar

Diversity raises the intelligence of groups.

Nancy Kline

Everything eventually becomes too high-priced.

Robert A Liston

It is not enough to succeed. Others must fail.

Gore Vidal